Drift boats are the general rule on c  ing by with only the creak of the oarlc of conversation or peal of laughter.

A guide boat with two anglers appear e oarsman rows steadily into the current in (...u steer it into a very specific position on the opposite ban ... une end of a gravel bar he drops the anchor in order to fish a spot where the water deepens and runs back into a slough. There is a definite seam where the swift water transitions to the calm. He puts fresh salmon eggs on for his customers and they drop their lines in the current and play them out slowly in a technique called back bouncing. One of the fisherman yells out excitedly as his pole bends sharply while the water explodes behind the boat with an airborne Silver Salmon surface to air missile. At the end of three dramatic leaps, the line goes slack. This fish will live to make it back to its spawning stream that feeds into Tustumena Lake. Hope for the future. Something we all need.

1994

Four of us have gotten together to charter the *Sea Verse III* for a full day with Captain Lee Severs. My friends Bruce Blair, Lionel Horne, my brother-in-law Bill Whitten and I have high hopes for the day. Captain Lee has a front line berth in Kewalo Basin and is one of the harbor's highliners-catching more fish than almost all of his peers. He has a large sign at the dock with the boat name, and on one of the posts supporting it is a cork board, enclosed in a locking glass case, which contains thirty or so Polaroid photos of recent catches with the dates written on the bottom. This is one of his best marketing tools. He has recently purchased his third charter fishing boat, a 42 foot Pacifica Yacht, and he is on a hot streak. I have fished with him on all three boats, and this new one is a dandy. Powered with twin Cummins diesels and boasting a flying bridge that accommodates five people, it is a fish catching machine.

We are idling out of the harbor at 6:00 a.m., well ahead of the other boats. His plan is to fish the standard itinerary for a full day charter. This consists of heading twenty miles southeast to the Fish Aggregating Device (FAD) known as HH Buoy and then turning west to BO Buoy which is located south of Barber's Point. We will be on the edge of the Molokai Channel on the way to HH and will scan the horizon for feeding seabirds or floating objects. As we leave the harbor I have a feeling that this will be a great day. It manifests as a warm tingling sensation on the back of my head, at the base of my neck.

It is early March, and dark for the first half hour, so Lee has his deckhand, John, run a single jet head lure with a glow stick attached three feet above the lure. At 6:30, dawn is creeping up on the port side of the boat with pink and yellow tendrils radiating into the pale blue sky. John gets out a deck of cards and we pick numbers out of a baseball cap to determine who will catch what, if a fish strikes. It is time to put out the lures.

"Charley, did you bring that lucky lure that you ran last time?"

"I did, skipper! I replaced the skirts that the ono shredded after it caught that big bull mahi."

Papa Tell Me A Story

Charley McCrone

Published by Charley McCrone, 2024.

PAPA TELL ME A STORY

First edition. February 24, 2024.

ISBN: 979-8224088218

Written by Charley McCrone.

Table of Contents

Prologue | This Is Where We Live Now...1

Clean Sweep!...4

Waimea Bay | A Magical Morning.. 12

Things Change 17

A Day to Remember 25

Kenai River Sockeye Salmon Fishing- Hawaii Style 41

Makua Kea'au..49

Fishing With Annette 62

Señoritas Fishing Tournament...75

Return To Prince of Wales... 81

Magic Bull Moment..112

Halibut on the Cheap..118

Reunion of the F/ V | Hoku O Ke Kai 125

The Best Time 134

Silvers of September..149

A Tale of Two Marlin 159

Epilogue..172

Papa Tell Me Another Story?...176

This collection of stories is dedicated to my muse, the Blushing Bride and mother of Charley's Angels.

She has inspired me to be much more than the man I would have otherwise been, and given me the freedom to have these adventures.

May these tales inspire our grandkids, and those who come after them, to pursue their passions and to live their dreams.

Prologue
This Is Where We Live Now

1994 When our girls were seven, nine and eleven years old, we took them to Sea Life Park across the road from Makapuu. It was quite an adventure. Always a joy to turn the corner after Koko Head and get that first glimpse of the Royal Blue waters of the Molokai Channel, usually frosted with whitecaps. On a clear day, Molokai, Maui and Lanai can be seen. We stop at the Halona Blowhole, and they love watching it shoot up spray like a whale made of lava. At the entrance to the several thousand gallon salt water aquarium, the artist Wyland is creating one of his world famous murals. It's serendipitous to be able to watch his artistic sorcery in person. After the aquarium with its incredible population of fish and *SHARKS* of all sorts, and the hokey Pirate/ Mermaid dolphin show, we sojourn down a path where there is an "authentic" recreation of a Hawaiian dwelling site with a thatched hut, fire pit, gourd water container and even a net on a drying rack. I took them inside and had them sit on the lauhala mat.

I asked them how they were enjoying the day, and then with all the solemnity I could muster, I told them, "Mommy and I sold the house, and this is where we live now."

One daughter looked pretty skeptical, one was ecstatic, and one started to cry.

2009

We bought the house on the River. Sitting in the living room, we can see the turquoise water sweep around a sharp bend on the right and flow down to disappear around another bend on the left. The swift current is framed by a solid wall of trees on both banks, the green spruce now contrasting with the ever-deepening golds of the birch and alders. Splashes of orange and red fireweed complete the canvas. I still can't believe we bought the house on the river.

She is the Kasilof -Kah-see-loff- little sister to the Mighty Kenai River, arguably the most famous salmon river in Alaska, or the world for that matter. We are fifteen miles away by car, but light-years removed from the congestion of power boats jockeying for position, float planes trying to land, and the infamous "combat fishing" of shore anglers trying to catch their limits of Red Salmon.

Tomorrow will make one week that we've been on the river, and only one boat with an outboard motor has gone by. Our Springer Spaniel, Hailey, barked menacingly at the shattering of our peaceful silence.

"Good girl, Hailey."

"Run it on the short outrigger John, and put out the same lures we had yesterday everywhere else."

The bait in question is one that I tied with a lure head given to me by Mr Valente, a next door neighbor to my wife when she was a little girl living in Makakilo. He is a big-hearted and generous Portuguese man with an ever-present smile and twinkling eyes. Originally from Kauai, he was an avid fisherman and lure maker. Annette tells me that he is an amazing gardener, with a citrus tree that has grafted branches of several varieties of fruits. He had a lemon tree of extra juicy lemons that never turned yellow, and Annette's mom used the juice to make the "best lemon meringue pies in the world." He also warned Annette not to eat the Hawaiian chili peppers that he grew, but when she saw that it was so attractive, with the waxy green and bright red peppers, she had to take a little bite. A very valuable lesson was learned. He also had two bushes of sweet-tart "Hawaiian Cherries" in the front yard that our girls thoroughly enjoyed. He and his wife made the most delicious crispy and spicy pickled vegetables. He taught me how to cook octopus to make it tender and tasty.

He once asked me, "Charley, do you know which star is the Portuguese star?"

"No," I replied.

"It's the 'not so bright one'..."

The first time I met him, I brought some freshly smoked marlin and a twelve pack of Olympia beer. He regaled me with stories of fishing the Kauai channel in his own boat, catching marlin and 'ahi in the rough waters. He showed me the lure heads he cast himself and invited me to pick one for myself. The sparkle in his eyes showed his approval of my selection.

This particular lure is designed to imitate a large malolo- a flying fish. The head is cast fiberglass, poured into a mold, over a cylindrical lead core, wrapped with silver reflective tape that radiates a rainbow of colors. The top half is tinted dark blue and the bottom is clear, with a yellow stripe in between. It has five copper tubes running through it, one for the leader and the others to create a bubble trail as it goes through the water. The face is flat and angled causing the lure to run erratically and pop out of the water every ten seconds or so. It has a two-toned outside skirt of frog patterned blue on top and solid silver colors on the bottom, which match the head colors identically. A blue and pink skirt with a yellow stripe is under it, and they cover a hot pink third skirt. The lure is finished off with wings of fish scale patterned Flecto paper that matches the silver reflective paper of the head. This is the second of four "magic" lures that I have known. They catch fish every time they are run, and sometimes are the only lure in the spread to do so. This lure contains some of Mr. Valente's *mana*.

John gets all of the lures out, and Lee has him adjust their distance—in closer or out farther—until he is satisfied with the spread. My magic lure is positioned to slide down the face of a wave and then dive underneath trailing a white stream of bubbles. The "Flower", an ice blue straight runner jet head, is on the long outrigger, and a smaller, angle cut chrome jet head, rigged with black salmon skirts over a purple glitter skirt, is on the center outrigger in what we call Never-Neverland, thirty yards past the long port outrigger. The long corner has a green Head Knocker lure that has a moving plastic cap which slides back and forth, making a tapping sound. The short starboard corner has an oversize Super Plunger scooped face lure creating a ruckus of large splashes, intended to attract fish from a distance. The center of the transom has a four inch lure, a silver chrome hex-head skirted with pink and blue. This lure catches our first fish, just as the sun is rising, a five pound skipjack tuna- aku in Hawaiian. We will *not* have a whitewash today. The sun is up now, and there is a hint of briskness as the wind freshens. The waves are a solid three feet, with an occasional higher crest. It is perfect trolling water.

The skipper is the first to see them. A small flock of boobies, gliding over the surface of the water and then climbing and changing direction. I finally locate them through the binoculars as Lee switches the autopilot off and turns into the waves. There are eight, and then ten birds in a fairly tight formation. They are occasionally dive-bombing the water, trapping baitfish between the birds above and the fish below. Lee maneuvers ahead of them and then crosses their path to present the lures perfectly. The magic lure is the first to be hit, and then a blue and silver streak is seen slicing across the face of a wave, attacking the Flower.

"Number one in the chair and number four on the fish box! Now!"

Lionel and Bill are first up, so Bruce and I help John to clear lines and get bait in the water in case there are followers. John is gaffing the first mahi at the same time Lionel's arrives, so I swing his into the box and shut the lid. Bill's fish comes aboard and we are able to get it in the box as well. There were no other fish behind, and the birds scatter, but we are happy to have caught dinner before 8:00 in the morning. Lee engages the autopilot again and reaches for his binoculars.

At 8:15 HH buoy comes into sight. There are no other boats in sight, so it looks like our early start was worthwhile. One shearwater is sitting atop the buoy and there are several others flying randomly in the vicinity, but no big piles. At 300 yards Lee begins making concentric circles around the FAD and at 200 yards we get another strike on Mr Valente's lure. It is strong, but not a screamer. In about five minutes a nice 20 pound yellowfin is led into the net. The fish was not big enough for us to reel in everything, so once it was landed we only had to reset the lucky lure. A pass right next to the buoy yields another strike. There seems to be a pattern here, with a very special lure. A fifteen pound ono is brought to the boat in a few minutes. When it is slid in the box, the skipper and I look at each other knowingly.

He raises his eyebrows and says, "If we catch a marlin, we'll have a clean sweep!"

Catching one or more of each species of pelagic fish is a rarity and a feather in the cap of whichever skipper accomplishes the feat.

"It's still early," I reply, and that tingling premonition of good things to come makes a return performance.

We make one more pass by the buoy and Lee yells at John to toss some chum at it as we close in. A cloud of trigger fish appears, and then he spots some green and yellow flashes.

"Reel in," he says "we're going to bait. Get Charley out."

"Charley" is a five pound aku from yesterday's trip with a 12/0 hook threaded through its lower and upper jaws, on a 300 pound test leader. A rubber band is wrapped around the hook and mouth to keep it shut. It is dropped back thirty yards behind the boat and the line is pulled at the crest of a swell to make it pop out of the water. Lee has a mackerel bait on a fifty pound class rod which is drifted out past the tuna. Three mahi appear behind the Charley and one inhales the bait. The reel is in free spool with the clicker on, and makes a high pitched buzzing sound as the fish swims away. After a count of five, the skipper engages the clutch and sets the hook.

"Hanapa'a!", he yells, "Get me another bait out!"

John has another bait ready in the cooler with the leader already attached to the second fifty pound bait rod. He flips it out down current as I take the rod Lee hands down from the bridge and give it to Bruce in the fighting chair. In less than minute, Lee hooks another and I get a turn to be the angler. My fish makes a series of impressive jumps, and then comes grudgingly to the boat where it is joined by Bruce's fish. We will be guaranteed to get some *kau-kau* fish with four mahi in the box. Everything got pretty quiet at the buoy after our flurry of action, so the skipper tells us to set up for trolling again.

Everything is run back out and adjusted, and it is very quiet on the boat. Blue water trolling has been very well described as hours of boredom, punctuated by moments of pandemonium. And the pandemonium is never guaranteed. There is a large flock of small birds spotted outside of us, and Lee tells John to get the handlines out. These are used primarily for smaller aku and consist of twenty to fifty feet of nylon cord attached to a four- foot length of surgical tubing. The line is fed through the tubing and a knot is made in the cord which is then secured by whipping it with heavy floss. The tubing is stretched over the line to its maximum length, where another knot is made and secured. When the tension is released, the cord coils up inside the tubing. The near end of the tubing has a large loop in the cord which is used to secure the handline to the stern cleat. When a fish strikes, the surgical tubing stretches, acting like a shock absorber, so the hook is not ripped out of the fish's jaw. Our handlines have the same hex heads dressed in pink and blue or pink and white skirts that caught our first fish. Lee maneuvers the boat alongside the flock of diving and flaring birds and we can see the aku slashing through the bait with their mouths open. The water boils where their prey is concentrated. The far end of the surgical tubing has been attached to the cleat with a rubber band so that the band breaks when a strike occurs. The center rod also has the main line rubber banded to the reel to keep the wind from blowing the line over and tangling and as a strike indicator. All three rubber bands break within a second of each other and we have three more tuna in the boat in about three minutes. They are about the same size as the first one we caught, and the skipper is not impressed. This is not the day to chase small tuna. He resets the autopilot for BO buoy, and we are on our way again.

An hour later, the FAD is in sight, and although there is no sign of bird life at the buoy itself, there is a small flock a few hundred yards away. Captain Lee heads toward them. These birds are flying rapidly and erratically, occasionally diving into the water. As we get closer, we see the forked tail of 'ahi birds. They are moving away from us and away from land, so Lee increases our speed to catch them. When he gets ahead of the flock, he drops back down to trolling speed and once again positions the lures in front of the fish without spooking them. It is more art than science. Thirty seconds later, the rod up on the flying bridge slams down- the small black salmon lure in Never-Neverland- and the 130 Shimano is screaming in protest. This is not a little tuna. Lionel is our designated angler on the fish, and we can tell from the type of birds and the behavior of the fish that we are tangling with a respectable size 'ahi. This Yellowfin Tuna hits like freight train and the first run is smoking line off the reel. Now it is straight down, deep below the boat, turning sideways to present the most resistance to being captured. It comes up slowly, in big circles until we can see the silver flash and sickle shaped golden fin. Lionel is slowly and steadily gaining line, and finally John is able to grasp the leader. Lee climbs down the ladder and places the first gaff expertly just below the gill plate. I assist with a second gaff and we slide it through the door. Then it's high fives all around! What an incredible day!

Lee bleeds the fish immediately and then guts and gills it. The next step is to chill it as quickly as possible by immersing it completely in an ice water bath in the fish box. Fish that are not properly bled and cooled bring a fraction of the price at auction, where this fish is destined to go. When this is done, we clean up and head to the buoy to try baiting before setting up to troll.

At the FAD, we redeploy Charley, and are successful in bringing three more mahi aboard. They are great eating size and a welcome addition to our bounty. It's nearly two o'clock, and time to start heading back to the harbor. I assist John in getting the trolling spread reset and adjust the lures to Lee's specifications. On the way back, our eagle-eyed Captain with the photo stabilizing binoculars spots another small flock of active birds closer to shore near Pearl Harbor. Lee tells John to replace the head knocker lure with a six inch jet head dressed with blue and silver skirts. Minutes after it is put out, the pole bends and in a few more minutes, we have a jumbo sized twelve-pound aku up to the boat. It is netted carefully and put in the box. This is an *otaru, a* prized fish for *sashimi* and *poke'* with a deeper red color flesh and a higher fat content than the smaller aku. We are getting some icing on our cake. The birds have moved on but are still within sight. These larger tuna are a rarity, and Lee is eager to pursue the school. He pushes the throttle forward to catch up to the school. The otaru move more rapidly than the smaller fish and can sound deeply if spooked. He is slowing the boat down when pandemonium ensues on the back deck. A marlin has launched into the air with Mr Valente's lure in its mouth and is now hell-bent for Maui. It was probably tracking the tuna school also, hoping to pick off a stray or two. The fish makes three amazing greyhounding leaps and then tail walks 150 yards behind the boat. My friend Bruce is in the chair- he is definitely the most experienced angler in our little group. He has placed twice in the Lahaina Jackpot Tournament and is well versed in catching trophy marlin. John assures that the line stays tight, with the rod still in the pole holder, while I help Bruce put on the fighting vest and remove the back from the chair. When the incredible first run slows, John brings the rod and slips the butt into the gimbal while I help to clip the straps on the reel. The fish is still taking line. The vest strapped to the reel allows Bruce to pull the fish forward simply by leaning back and using the footrest and his weight. When the rod is almost straight up, he retrieves the line smoothly by reeling and keeping tension while lowering the rod tip. The fish is halfway in when it makes another strong run but does not jump. In another ten minutes, the leader is coming up and Lee clambers down from the bridge. The rope on the flying gaff is tied to the bottom of the chair, and two other gaffs are standing by. Lionel is at the controls and Lee tells him to throttle down while John grasps the pigtail swivel and takes his first wraps on the 300 pound test leader. The 10/0 hook is caught perfectly in the corner of the marlin's jaw. John takes his final wrap and walks toward the bow as Lee slips into place with the big gaff. He plants it solidly behind the shoulder and the hook releases from the handle. I set another gaff in the gill plate, and Lee uses a mallet to administer the death blow. The mighty fish lights up with a brilliant neon blue and silver display of color for a moment and then slowly fades. There is a tinge of melancholy mingled with the exhilaration of catching a fish like this.

John puts down a tarp and we slide the marlin on it, then pour two fifty pound bags of ice into four wet burlap bags which are placed on the fish to chill it as quickly as possible. The tarp is tied up over it afterwards. The rest of the trip back was uneventful. John runs all five flags up the outrigger line at the head buoy. Lionel's 'ahi comes in at just under a hundred pounds, and Bruce's marlin at a very healthy two hundred and fifty pounds. We attract quite a crowd back at the harbor, including some very envious crews from the other charter boats. Lee got to take the marlin and 'ahi, and the two largest mahi to the auction. He also got a polaroid on his cork board that keeps him booked for the rest of the month.

Just before we left, he asked, "Charley, when are you going to give me that lure?"

"I'll give it to you when I quit fishing, skipper. Don't hold your breath."

We get to share the rest of the fish equally with the crew, which exceeds our expectations. But the best part of the experience is to be able to look at the old photos and enjoy the memory of this day for the rest of our lives. The day we got the Clean Sweep!

Waimea Bay
A Magical Morning

1996 It is early September. The days are becoming noticeably shorter, and the mornings are chilly-especially after the humid dog days of August. Juvenile baitfish are schooling in the shallow waters all around the island. The most prolific and popular, are the o'ama, or baby goatfish. They are joined in the waters of Waimea Bay by halalu- adolescent akule or bigeye scad, young opelu- mackerel scad, and tiny stickfish—aha in Hawaiian. Schools vary in size from a few dozen to thousands of fish. The baitfish are eagerly pursued by fish and fishermen alike.

"Who wants to go to Waimea tomorrow morning?" It was a rhetorical question.

"We do, we do!" was the immediate and emphatic answer from Kris and Kelly.

Shannon is going to the movies with Anela and Jennie from the block. Our girls have been water babies from the time that they were toddlers.

"If you don't come out of the water RIGHT NOW, you're not going to the beach next week!" was the only way to extricate them from the water.

We needed to get to the beach by 7:00 am if we were going to find a parking spot in the lot on a weekend, even in the late 1980s, so I packed up all of the gear and told the girls we would be leaving at six in the morning.

"You can sleep on the way down."

6:45 finds us going down the big hill and turning into our destination. It is clear and cold, which means it will be sunny and warm in a few hours. We clamber out of the truck and at the end of the grass, take off our slippers and put them in one of the buckets. The damp cool sand feels great on my feet. We carry our gear down to a spot just to the left of where the stream empties into the bay. Waimea translates as "red water". After a heavy rain the stream rages with bright red clay sediment giving the bay its name. There are two five gallon buckets with all of the fishing gear, including a battery powered aerator, one each large and small spinning rods, a sand spike rod holder and two fiberglass six foot straight rods without reels for catching bait. A small red scoop net, a cooler, and snorkeling gear for the girls creates an impressive load. There are already a dozen rods in the water and dozens more on the way. A small cluster of people are standing knee deep in the water halfway between us and the Jumping Off Rock to the left. They are catching the four inch long oama.

"Let's catch some bait, girls!"

I pull out a small one gallon bucket from the larger one, a can of mackerel and a can opener. The fish is mixed thoroughly with about three fourths of a bucket of sand for our palu. The bait catching rods have six feet of two pound test line, a tiny number sixteen hook and a single split shot weight about four inches above the hook. Kris and Kelly are at the water's edge and are pointing.

"Over here, dad— we see some."

There is a slight shimmer of the ghost like forms of oama out about ten feet from them. They grab their rods and are ready for action. I get a few handfuls of the sandy chum and put it in a small plastic grocery bag which is tied loosely to the string on the waist of my bathing suit. The small red scoop net with tiny mesh is tucked into my bathing suit as well. We wade out to knee deep into the water and I toss a small handful of the palu toward the few fish that we see. They smell it in a few seconds and are drawn closer. In another minute I toss a little more sand closer to us and they are in range of our poles. Before long the school grows to several dozen fish eating the tiny bits of mackerel. The girls are standing on either side of me and I bait their hooks with a piece of shrimp the size of a rice grain. They are taught to watch when the white shrimp disappears to lift the rod and drop the fish right into my net. Kelly gets the first one and Kris is right behind her. Two flip off on the way to the net and very quickly I have four. I wade to shore, drop three of them in the bait bucket and turn on the aerator. The fourth is hooked on a number twenty six BKN circle hook with a four foot twenty pound test leader and a four ounce weight, then cast out about thirty yards from shore. I attach my favorite bell on a rod eye, just above my head. One of the fishermen on our left catches a papio of about three pounds and another rod further to the left bends down sharply.

Our activity with the oama has not gone unnoticed, and four people want to become our new best friends. The girls catch another half dozen fish and then the school seems to take roll call and heads back to deeper water. After the oama leave, a group of tiny stick fish swarm into the chum slick. The girls take off the split shot weight and fly fish with the unweighted shrimp. The little baitfish attack the drifting offering like miniature marlin, charging in at full speed, running to the end of the line and flying into the air. We keep a few of them for bait and then the girls want to go snorkeling.

A shifting cloud of halalu is spotted about a hundred yards from shore and a small group of anglers watches the school with the intensity of a shark. The girls will swim out to them, fascinated by the way the fish swirl and dart through the water in perfect unity. When a predator fish, or school of fish attacks, they explode in a chaotic display of energy, diving deeply and jumping out of the water. On rare occasions our girls have been able to swim among the Spinner Dolphin school that used to frequent the bay quite often. It is an unforgettable experience to see them from the shore, surfing in the swells and doing multiple 360 degree airborne acrobatic maneuvers. It is even more exciting to be snorkeling next to them.

"If the halalu get within casting distance from shore, make sure you stay away. The fishermen get angry when you chase the school of fish and I don't want you getting hooked. I'm not sure what the legal limit is for catching haole girls..."

They swim around the school of little mackerel until the fish are close enough for the eager group of fishermen to cast over them. The setup for catching the six inch fish is a petite sized spinning reel loaded with four pound test line, a one half to one ounce lead, a six to ten foot leader of two pound test line and a small "ah" hook with a translucent two inch plastic strip- usually a lime green or clear color. Some fishermen use tiny curly tails or strips cut from clear plastic gloves. The setup is cast over the school and allowed to sink for a second or two and then retrieved in a rapid series of sweeping motions of the rod. The technique is called "whipping" for obvious reasons. Few of these fish are used for bait; they are prized for eating either fried or as kinilaw- a version of ceviche. No big fish are coming in, so I put a fresh bait on the big pole and join the little group who are targeting the halalu. They are catching some, and there is an interesting contrast in techniques. Varying speeds of retrieval and different angles and frequency of rod motions. Successful anglers are mimicked in an attempt to get hookups. The fish are so small that it can be difficult to tell when they are hooked, but when it happens the retrieval speed is slowed and the line is retrieved carefully.

This school of fish works its way down the beach and to the left, in and out. Suddenly the cloud has a large hole in the center and fish are exploding in a volcanic eruption. Some unseen predators have panicked them. They move further to the left, getting close to the Jumping Off Rock. Shortly after, there is a shoreline blitz with rods bending and fishermen jumping in a definite sequence up from the rock all the way to the stream. Nothing is happening on my pole. I come back to put a few halalu in the cooler and change bait. Kelly is resting after two hours in the water, but Kris wants to stay in the shallows and look for shells in the shore break trench. I tell her to stay close and ask Kelly to watch our stuff, then head back to the action. About ten minutes later I am surprised by a Japanese woman tapping me on the shoulder. She is one of our new friends from the oama party earlier this morning.

"Your daughter is fighting a very big fish and it looks like it has taken out a lot of line!" I thank her and spot Kelly with the heavily bent rod and start jogging down the beach on the hardened damp sand. She is doing a great job, but is happy to see me.

"It's *REALLY BIG* dad!"

She hands me the pole and I can feel the weight and power of this fish. The long ripping run slows and I am able to turn its head and slowly work it toward the beach. When the fish is in the shore break it makes one last powerful run and then yields to the steady pressure. I surf it in on a wave and then slide it up out of the surge zone. The circle hook is lodged solidly in the corner of its mouth. Kris has heard all of the commotion and joins us on the beach where we all do a little happy dance. It is a kawa-kawa one of the most prized tunas in Hawaii, and my personal favorite for sashimi. It is also excellent for grilling, basted with lemon and butter and cooked medium rare. I bleed it by cutting the gills and then rinse it and put it in the cooler. The tail is sticking out so I tell the girls that we have to go home.

"But dad, we want to swim some more. *PLEASE* dad??"

"Okay, ten more minutes, but then we have to go get some more ice."

After fifteen minutes I call them out and they pretend not to hear me.

"If you don't come out of the water RIGHT NOW..."

• • • •

1996 It is Saturday, the 3rd of July. Six of us have a charter date with Captain Lee Severs on the *Sea Verse lll*. We are hoping for a fresh fish dinner to celebrate the fourth of July. Most tourists who go charter fishing don't have any interest in keeping their fish because they don't have the means to process and freeze it. Being local residents, we want fish to eat. I have arranged with the skipper to charge whatever price he needs for the boat based on allowing us to keep half of whatever is caught. We like fish. A lot. A big part of the income stream for charter boats is the sale of fish. Some may go to a restaurant, if the captain has a good relationship with the owner, but the majority goes to the Honolulu Fish Auction. The standard division, if the skipper owns his boat, is that the deckhand(s) get one third of the proceeds from fish sales, the boat gets one third and the skipper gets the last share. Tips, and/or any income that comes from selling fiberglass mounts of fish caught are split fifty-fifty.

Captain Lee calls me on Friday to confirm.

"There's been a lot of 'ahi coming up off of Waianae this week, so we should leave early and head straight there in the morning. It's a long run, so have everyone at the boat by 5:30."

"Okay fine, skipper. We'll be there." I call everyone, and tell them to be there by 5:15. If you're not there, you still have to pay..."

Everyone is on time, and we are steaming out of Kewalo Basin just as the sun is peeking over the horizon and melting away the morning mist. It is dead calm and clear with just a few puffs of clouds. We have two deckhands today, and one gives us a briefing as we head out of the harbor while the other attaches lures to the rods. As soon as we clear the head buoy, the captain points us toward Barber's Point and sets the autopilot. The trolling speed seems just a knot or two faster than usual. Captain Lee is on a mission. When the giant 'ahi, of 100 pounds and up run, it is possible to have multiple hookups at one time and then follow the school to end the day with double digit catches. These yellowfin tuna are frequently accompanied by terns—usually sooty terns—'ewa 'ewa in Hawaiian. They are similar to aku birds, but have a white breast, forked tails and travel in much smaller flocks than the noddies. They are much more erratic in their flight pattern, darting quickly, and then instantly changing direction to capture the bait that the 'ahi are pursuing. Typically, when the birds are spotted, the captain passes them on the side in an effort to position the boat so that the lures intersect the path of the fish without getting close enough to spook them. Novice weekend warrior fishermen sometimes blast right through the birds and into the school. The fish are never seen again.

After two hours of scanning barren blue water, the sight of a few 'ahi birds turning into a small flock and their flight patterns indicating that they are on fish, can cause the hair to stand up on the back of my neck in anticipation. When the tuna find a school of baitfish, they can often corral them into a whirling bait ball and then take turns leaping into the air, with their sickle shaped golden fins flashing, then crashing through the bait.

"'AHI BUSTING!!!" is the clarion call when it is seen. It is often followed by two or more rods screaming in protest as line races off the spool. It is an unforgettable off-the-chart, goosebump creating experience. When native Hawaiians fished for them with hand lines made of coconut husk fiber, the initial run could be so fast and hard that the line would set the edge of the outrigger canoe on fire. 'Ahi is the Hawaiian word for fire. After the first run the fish dive deep down and slug it out, turning their broad bodies sideways to the direction they are being pulled, causing the angler to work hard for every inch of line retrieved. They come up in wide circles, grudgingly, and almost always make one last dash just before being brought to the boat. I fully understand the skipper's excitement to pursue these fish exclusively. This "full day, eight hour charter" may well turn into twelve or more hours if we are successful.

We are passing Pearl Harbor and I am scanning the water with binoculars when I spot a large flock of noddies- aku birds- drifting in an ever-shifting cloud and moving slowly away from us. Some begin to circle and pile up in a concentration and then dive into the water. They are following a school of skipjack tuna, typically four to six pounds in weight, and eating whatever the tuna feast on.

"Aku birds at ten o'clock, skipper."

"No aku birds today." he replies quickly.

There is a popular bumper sticker on Oahu that says simply "No Aku Birds". The most common explanation is that an "aku bird" is a moocher who brings potato chips to a party and drinks all the beer and eats all the food. This is based on the idea that the noio follow the tuna and then feast on the bait that is trapped by the fish and driven to the surface, without contributing anything. Captain Lee simply means that we aren't going to use any of our precious time chasing small tuna when we could be catching giant 'ahi.

7:45 and we are right at the tip of Barber's Point, about three miles offshore. The point is always rougher than the adjacent waters, and we are now coming into the beginning of marlin and 'ahi territory. There are whitecaps and bumpy three foot swells, but we can see the nearly calm waters of the leeward side ahead.

"High flier, Lee, at nine o'clock. There's two, no three, white birds underneath."

The high flier is an 'Iwa, or great frigate bird with a six foot wingspan. It will take a big deal for Lee to deviate from his course this morning, but the 'Iwa with three boobies *is* a big deal. This bird is known to follow large game fish like marlin or tuna and feast on the remains of whatever they eat. 'Iwa is the Hawaiian word for thief. They cannot land on the water and must snatch their food without doing so. They are often seen badgering other birds with their beaks, causing them to disgorge what they have eaten, in order to feed themselves. That is how they earned the moniker of man-of-war-bird. Any time we see one gliding effortlessly at 300 feet in the air while trolling, Lee will make a pass underneath to see if we can entice a strike. To see one descend rapidly is a sure sign that something seriously fishy is happening. After confirming what I said with his image-stabilizing binoculars, I can see the skipper struggling mentally for a moment, and then he flips a switch, to retire our German pilot named Otto, temporarily.

"An 'Iwa with white birds underneath is almost always a school of mahimahi" he says.

Still watching through my binoculars, I reply "The 'Iwa is coming down!"

Our two deckhands are on the flying bridge with us. Darrel 1 is studying Coast Guard regulations in anticipation of taking his test to become a licensed Captain, while Darryl 2 has been inspecting the inside of his eyelids for leaks. They both suddenly come to life and scramble down the stairs.

"Deckhands are either great or terrible, and neither of them stays for very long" Lee says as they leave. "The good ones become captains and get their own boats, and the bad ones screw up one too many times and get fired."

That is how I transitioned from being a customer to working part-time as a member of the crew. Lee called on a Friday night a week before Christmas.

"I had to fire my deckhand today; he got drunk and shot off a flare gun in the harbor last night. I need somebody for charters I have booked tomorrow and Sunday. Can you come and fish with me?"

It was music to my ears, and the blushing bride graciously gave her blessing. She likes Lee a lot better than my previous fishing partner.

Meanwhile, back at the birds, we are about 500 yards away and closing in quickly. There are a dozen birds-white boobies and gray and white shearwaters, circling a small area and not drifting away from it.

"Looks like a floater!" our skipper says.

Floating objects in the open ocean attract schools of baitfish which, in turn, attract predators. These are most commonly mahi mahi, ono, and small aku and/or 'ahi. Occasionally the giant 'ahi will hang out for a little while, and a big log or sheet of plywood can have a marlin lurking about to bushwhack small tuna. As we get closer, I can see something very long and brown as the swell crests in the distance.

"It's a net!" Lee says. "And it looks like a sea of blue and green all around it!"

At a hundred yards out Lee turns the boat to make a slow lazy circle around the floater to see if we can get a strike from any large tuna or marlin. The concentric circles are getting closer to the net when all hell breaks loose on the back deck as six poles go off at once. Emerald green and golden, then turning silver and blue, mahi are jumping everywhere, crossing and tangling lines in complete and total chaos. The whole ocean around the net seems alive with hundreds of fish in a cloud, shifting back and forth. Lee turns the boat away from the school as everyone is reeling in fish from the rod holders.

"Get them in as soon as you can, and then stow the 130s in the cabin and get everything ready to bait!" Lee yells from the bridge.

Five of the six make it into the fish box, and the 130 pound class poles are hung up in the cabin. There are two 50 pound class Shimanos on the bridge for baiting, having leaders that run into the cooler that is nestled between the ladder that leads to the bridge and the wall of the cabin. They have razor sharp 9/0 bait hooks running through the upper and lower jaws of saba-mackerel. Lee buys the fish in 25 pound boxes. We have two gallon bags of them in the bait cooler along with two aku and a gallon bag of anchovies used for chum. The bulkhead above the cooler has thirty coiled six foot long leaders of 150 pound test mono hanging up. We are ready to go. Lee barks instructions.

"Set up the two fifties on the corners with an eighty pound class in the center. Numbers one, two and three start out. As soon as you get your fish in, or lose it, numbers four five and six are up. Darryl and Darrel will leader and flip fish in the box. Charley, you are in charge of having fresh leaders baited and icing the fish. Get your boys to help. Does everybody understand?"

Lee positions the boat up current from the net so that we drift back slowly toward it while the deckhands drift the baited hooks behind the boat on the port and starboard corners. I am assigned to the center. The silence is broken when all three reels make a high pitched buzzing sound simultaneously. The reels are in free spool with the clickers on and a light thumb on the spool assures that the line doesn't backlash. We have been instructed to count one-thousand-one up to five before engaging the clutch. When we do, the water behind the boat becomes the stage for an airborne aquarian ballet with fish jumping in all directions. These mahi are a respectable size, in the fifteen to twenty pound range, but we are not gaffing them. They are instead flipped directly into the smaller of two fish boxes on the boat. The box is on the starboard stern and is two feet square and six feet long. It has fifty pounds of crushed ice and five gallons of water, with the addition a cup of rock salt to cause the ice to melt quickly and create a brine that will chill and kill the fish quickly. The cover is hinged at two feet so that a four foot section can be lifted to allow fish to be put in, and then closed immediately, while the fish goes through its dance of the pyramids on the way to mahimahi heaven, where flying fish abound and the sea is full of squid. The second fish box is three feet high, two feet wide and six feet long. It has a removable fiberglass top and a cushioned pad on top for seating. It's got seven fifty pound bags of ice—the eighth is in the smaller box—and is covered with an insulated fish bag that can also be used for storage. My job, as long as the frenzy continues, is to unhook and bleed the incoming fish by cutting at the base of the gills, then take the first fishes caught from the bottom of the box and stack and ice them in the big box.

All three of the fish on bait are welcomed aboard. The leaders are detached from the swivels as soon as the fish are in the box and replaced with freshly baited ones. Darryl is now in charge of hooking the fish one at a time from the port corner down current, and our other Darrel has the responsibility of piping the fish aboard on the starboard corner. The skipper is using the engines to keep the boat right on the edge of the school, against the current, without spooking the fish. We are not exactly a well-oiled machine, but the fish are coming aboard steadily. We have been using half of a mackerel for bait, and the supply is running low.

"Charley, get a box of ika from the freezer and soak it in a bucket of water" Lee says.

There is a small freezer in the bow stateroom and I grab the five pound box. I thrust the bucket underwater and pull it aboard, then rip off the cardboard packaging and immerse the block of squid. A handful of rock salt is added to increase the salinity and speed the thawing process. Then it's back to baiting hooks and stacking fish. Many of them have swallowed the hook and sometimes it can be removed by reaching into the gill with pliers to access it. The number of new hooks left above the bait cooler is dwindling, so we need to retrieve as many as we can. Pat and Kenny are helping me stack fish in the big box. They are placed belly down and head to tail in an alternating pattern and ice is packed in between so that they don't chafe. If they rub together with the rocking of the boat and lose scales, they will bring a much lower price at auction. Half of the ice has been used already, and mahi are still coming over the rail steadily. Water is sloshing out of the small box, so I pull the drain plug and a gurry of bloody liquid flows out of the box and out through the scuppers. We add another fifty pounds of ice, a bucket of water and salt. Everyone is sweating. The entire drama that has been unfolding since the initial explosion of excitement when all the rods were hit, has had a dream like, surreal feel to it. The initial chaos has evolved into a system where each person knows and performs their role. We have morphed into a fish harvesting vessel, and each of us is appreciating how unique and special this experience is. It is very unusual for everyone on a charter fishing trip to catch even one fish, let alone multiples. Many times a full day trip can be nothing more than a long, boring and hot boat ride.

The frozen squid is thawing, and I peel them off the outside of the block carefully and insert the hook twice at the tip and place them in the bait cooler. Then we pull another four fish from the bottom of the pile in the small box and stack and ice them carefully in the big box. Lather, rinse repeat. We have been pulling fish aboard steadily for five hours.

"I just finished the last bag of ice, skipper, and we only have a few more baits left."

"How many fish do we have?" is the response.

"Lots!"

"Bring everything in, get cleaned up, and set us up for trolling."

The mahimahi are still hitting the bait steadily, and there appears to be very little difference in the size of the school or their eagerness to bite. But enough is enough, and we all feel blessed to have been able to share this experience. The memory of this day will always bring a smile to our faces.

The trip back didn't produce any fish or strikes, and now we are tied up at the dock, unloading the fish. They just keep magically coming out of the box, and as they increase so does the number of onlookers. Passersby and crews from the other boats look on with envy. A tourist bus stops and unloads, and lots of folks are taking pictures. Afterwards comes the moment of truth. *FIFTY FOUR FISH!*

I get my truck and lay down a tarp on the bed. Lee and I jun-ken-po for first choice, and then we take turns picking fish. They are nearly identical in size, so it becomes humorous after a while. We all pitch in to get a generous tip for the captain and crew. Then it's a quick stop at the auction house to get the fish covered in ice and tie the tarp down over them. It's time to head home. Back at the ranch, we clean fish for a solid two hours and divide them evenly. Nobody dreamed that we would end up with such a bounty. The miracle Jesus performed for Peter was ninety nine more, exactly, but they weren't mahimahi. We will all have fresh fish for the Fourth of July, and for a long time afterwards...

On Monday afternoon I got a call from the captain. "The next time we go out, your group can have half of the fish up to a hundred pounds, but we get to keep anything over that."

"Okay fine, skipper. I understand. It was good while it lasted."

Things change...

A Day to Remember

2000 It is 4:15 on a Friday, and we are forty-five minutes into our ride home from a tile job in Waikiki. We're crawling up Red Hill in the usual Friday slow motion procession, with another solid half hour to go, when my phone goes off. The caller id reads "Captain Lee". I smile. . .

"Are you free on Sunday?" The Skipper never wastes words.

"No, but I'm relatively inexpensive", I answer.

"I've got a full day exclusive on Sunday with a group who have a wedding on Saturday, if you want to crew for me. You can bring your daughter along as an assistant deckhand if you want."

A tingling begins somewhere south of my solar plexus and produces a wide grin on my face. My disposition has just transcended the frustration of traffic, work responsibilities and irritations with customers and employees.

"I will call you back tonight, after I talk to the blushing bride" I tell him. I know that I'm the boss in the family, because she said so, but I don't make commitments without talking to her first. Happy spouse, happy house. The opposite is also true

About an hour later. . .

"What time do you want us there?"

"I told them 6:15, so you should be there at 5:45; get the rods out and wipe down the cushions. I'll be there at 6:00 with the ice. There have been some Mahi coming in so we will try to be first on the buoy."

"Okay fine, Skipper; we'll see you then", it was a thirty second men's conversation.

At 3:57 am on Sunday I punch the off button on the alarm after a fitful night of checking the time almost hourly. It is much too early. I check to make sure the programmed coffee maker is working and rouse Kris. She is not a morning person, but gets up immediately. After the morning ablutions are completed, I check the marine forecast. They are calling for fifteen knot winds in the morning with four foot seas, and four to six footers in the afternoon. I grab my little brown plastic utility box with a handle in the middle and open compartments on each side. One side has five large lures and a hookless teaser in

25

the shape of a flying fish. The other side has my binoculars, sunglasses, hat and several small lures with leaders in sandwich baggies for small tuna- aku, kawa kawa and little 'ahi. A sack with a couple of two liter water bottles, two large cans of Arizona Tea and a couple of frozen beef and bean burritos make up the mainstay of our provisions for the day. 4:30 finds us bound for Kewalo Basin and the boat. Taking the Kinau Street exit we head down Ward Avenue making a quick pass through the Jack In The Box drive-thru for two Breakfast Jacks. Left on Ala Moana Boulevard, and we make the first right after the harbor to access the free parking at Magic Island. You have to hang a u-turn in order to be facing out or deal with the consequences of spending an extra fifteen minutes driving out through the whole length of the park after a long day of fishing. It is dark and damp as we patter across the grass, clamber over the cement block wall and make it to the boat. Right on time.

The *Sea Verse III* is a forty six foot Pacifica Yacht, recently repowered with twin 555 Cummins diesel engines. She is a beauty. The original *Sea Verse* and *Sea Verse II* were both what were called "Haole Sampans". Built in the style of the Japanese fishing boats but modified to have full sized cabins. The flying bridge seats five comfortably, and the main cabin is spacious with a comfortable head and a private cabin. More importantly, she is a "Lucky Boat" with a reputation of attracting and not repelling fish. Fishermen are a superstitious lot.

I retrieve the key from its hiding place under the fighting chair seat cushion and unlock the sliding glass door into the cabin. The rods are all hung on the ceiling- five 130 Internationals, one 80 and two 50 pound class for bait rods. We put them in their places, but the two corner rods on the back deck angle out, so they are put into their traveling positions until we clear the harbor. The bait rods and one 130 go up on the flying bridge. Then we wipe the condensation from the outside seats as the skipper pulls up with eight fifty pound bags of ice. We open the large ice box on the back deck and stow them as Lee checks fluid levels. The engines roar to life and then begin that rhythmic diesel chugging sound. I stick the breakfast sandwiches and frozen burritos on one of the the engine manifolds and Lee puts two foil wrapped packets on the other.

Our charters arrive ten minutes early in a pair of taxis, and we ask them to wait a New York minute as we finish getting everything squared away. They are the fathers of the bride and groom, three younger guys, and one looks like an uncle. I unload the bait cooler and the captain parks his truck in the harbor lot that requires an expensive "K" sticker. He greets the prospective anglers and says "Welcome aboard; we are ready."

Then I stand by the steps and greet them "Good morning and welcome aboard. That's Captain Lee up on the flying bridge. My name is Charley, and I will be your deckhand today. This is my daughter Kris, and she will be our assistant deckhand." They come on board and I say "Make yourselves comfortable; here is a built in ice box in the cabin to store your food and drinks. We will have a briefing as soon as we clear the harbor and get the lines set."

I take the spring line off the cleat and lay it on the pier, Kris unhooks the stern lines and I untie the starboard bowline and hang it on the piling for easy retrieval when we return. I untie the port line and look to Captain Lee. He gives me the thumbs up; I hang it on the edge of the dock, and we are clear and off. He pulls out then reverses and turns and we are idling next to all of the other front line charter boats. There are several yellow mahi mahi flags, an assortment of green aku flags and one blue marlin pennant flying off the outriggers of the resting boats. Some of the deck lights are on with crews prepping, but we are the first out of the harbor again. Lee bumps the throttles up to trolling speed. I am setting the corner rods in their angled positions and as we pass the breakwater I set out a lone lure on the starboard corner, back about fifty yards. Occasionally there will be a mahi or ono hanging out at the head buoy marking the end of the channel. The outriggers come out of their upright positions and are locked into place. I take off the mahi and tuna flags from the last trip out, fold them and stow them in the cabinet.

Nobody is home at the head buoy, so I crank the corner in up to the end of the leader. Then it's up the ladder to ask the big question.

"What do you want to run today?"

"Put the Black Salmon on the center rigger and run whatever else you want."

That is always my favorite answer. Today's menu will have Lee's lucky lure on the furthest distance from the boat. It caught two mahi on the last trip, and a hundred pound 'ahi earlier in the month. The lure has a small, angled chrome jet head, with a skirt that is dark on top and bluish gray underneath. The inside skirt is a reddish purple with black glitter. It has red beaded eyes, wings of silver reflective paper and a single 10/0 bait hook. The total length is about nine inches. On the long outrigger I am running another chrome jet head. Lee named it the Flower, "because it's so pretty". It has a rounded bullet shaped head with four holes that create a bubble trail as it runs. The story is that the original Jet Head Lure was crafted from a Kona fisherman's old shower head. This lure has an outside skirt of ice blue- a transparent light blue with glitter. Under that is a bright yellow and finally a fluorescent hot pink skirt. This lure also has wings. They are a narrow, pointed strip of silver reflective paper that has a fish scale pattern. The reflection creates a rainbow of colors in the sunlight. It has two 10/0 bait hooks rigged in tandem, one facing up and one down. This utility lure catches every species of flag fish regularly and is a staple in the lineup. The short 'rigger will have my favorite lure. It is a Dennis Odagiri fiberglass head, blue fish scale pattern above and silver below with a thin yellow stripe between. It has large red eyes as well. The face is flat and angled to cause the lure to pop above the surface in a rhythm. It also has four copper tubes running through it to create a bubble trail. The outside skirt is a frog skin pattern blue/silver that matches the color of the head exactly. Under that is a blue/silver with a yellow stripe and the inside skirt is purple glitter. The wings on this lure are about six inches long. This bait has caught every species of flag fish and is sometimes the only one to catch anything. The long corner will have a new addition to our offering. It is a twelve inch long hookless teaser. An anatomically correct airbrushed fiberglass molded flying fish with aluminum wings that skitters over the surface of the water. A nine inch straight runner jet head lure, skirted with blue and silver over blue and pink is attached to run fifteen feet behind it. It has a single 9/0 bait hook. The short corner has a giant sixteen inch plunger type lure that imitates a tuna. The concave head is made to constantly push big splashes of water creating a ruckus on the surface which attracts curious fish. It has two 12/0 hooks and can entice giant marlin and fifty pound bull mahi mahi to come right up next to the boat. The last lure, on the center short position is a clear fiberglass head with a real fish head cast inside. It is colored black on top, so it is skirted with two black and silver skirts and a pink inside skirt. The wings are made from the dried skin of a lai that match the dried skin on the lure head. As I lay out the lures on the fighting chair in preparation, I get a tingling feeling from my neck and then down my back. It feels like it's going to be a day to remember.

Kris is up on the flying bridge, and I ask her to drop down the line from the International 130 pound reel. The lucky lure from yesterday is attached and let out behind the boat. I clamber up the ladder, put the reel in free spool, and with my thumb lightly on the spool to prevent a backlash, count "one thousand one" up to sixty. Dawn is breaking, but it is too dark to see the lure. The line is clipped into the center outrigger roller troller clip and run up to the end of the outrigger. Then it's down to the deck and the long outrigger, on the downwind side of the boat is run out to a count of fifty. Short 'rigger forty, long corner thirty, short corner twenty and the center is at fifteen seconds. My job is to separate the lines so that they don't get tangled. The skipper's job is to tangle them by turning abruptly or choosing light lures on the upwind side that get blown across the others. Unfortunately, he wins occasionally. The worst tangles can occur when there are multiple strikes-especially fish that jump like mahimahi or striped marlin. But I digress... Captain Lee sets the GPS to the coordinates for HH Buoy and engages the autopilot. The buoy is a FAD - fish aggregation device- anchored to the sea floor. It attracts bait fish which, in turn, attract the larger predators. The skipper pulls out his stabilizing binoculars and scans the horizon. When he presses a button, they create a momentary image that can be studied without the distracting movement of the boat interfering. We should be at the buoy in about two and a half hours.

"Okay, everybody, the lines are set, let's get together for the briefing.

"Thank you for choosing to go out with us today! We will do our best to get you on some fish. Again, my name is Charley, that's Captain Lee up there driving the boat"-he turns with a smile and waves- "and this is my daughter Kris. First things first- the head is located in the bow. To use it for number one, just push the button when you are done. For number two, flush it before using it, and then in shifts, and only use a small amount of toilet paper. If it gets plugged we will lose valuable fishing time dealing with the situation. If you are feeling seasick, do not go into the head. It is the worst possible place to be. Go to the back deck, hold on with both hands and call out for the friend you left behind- 'Ralph'. Most people feel much better afterwards. If you want to consume alcoholic beverages on board, please do so responsibly." At this point, I pass around a baseball cap with folded slips of paper which are numbered one to six. "Your number indicates which fishing pole is yours. Number one is the starboard outrigger and we go around clockwise to the starboard corner for number two and so on until number six ends at the center outrigger. When a fish strikes, I will yell out a number and your job is to make your way to the fighting chair as quickly and safely as possible. I will remove the rod from the holder and place the butt into the gimbal on the front of the chair. If there are two or more hookups the higher numbers are to go to the poles and reel to keep the lines tight until I give you more directions. You may have noticed that I said 'when' the fish bites, not if... It may be this morning, it may be this afternoon, or it may be tomorrow. This is fishing, and there are no guarantees. Except in Alaska. If we reel in the lures and fish with bait, number one will be first to fight any fish that is hooked, and so on. The most important consideration for us today, though, is safety. We do have life jackets upstairs under the seats if anyone would like to wear one. The water is pretty calm this morning, but as we get further out there will be some rocking and rolling. Try to always maintain three points of contact to avoid falling. If you are not the angler when a fish is hooked up, please clear the back deck and go into the cabin, or up on the flying bridge. Upstairs is a good place to take pictures of the action. If you are the angler, stay in the fighting chair and keep your feet up on the step at all times. There are very sharp hooks and gaffs that are in use, and we don't want to have any mishaps. If you are the angler, your job is to keep this rod, with the flexibility of a broomstick, bent at all times. The technique for catching a large pelagic gamefish is to pull the fish forward and then crank the reel while dropping the rod tip, maintaining a steady pressure all the way down. The number one reason for lost fish is a slack line which allows them to spit the hook. The reel drags are set to a tension that allows the fish to take line before the hook will pull out, if it is hooked solidly. If the fish wants to run, just hold onto the rod and wait until the run ends to begin retrieval. Also, these reels don't have a line guide, so it is necessary for you to guide the line back and forth with your free hand if there is a lot of line taken on the initial run. Don't be overwhelmed; we will help you with that. When you have reeled the fish up to the leader, our job begins. Hold the rod firmly, in case the fish pulls hard enough that we feel we must let the leader go. The fish will be netted or gaffed at the boat, and when it is secured in the fish box, we will take the rod from you. Any questions, and does anyone want to sit in the chair and practice reeling?" Usually, two or three people will do this, and it is good for the inexperienced anglers to get a feel for the heavy rods and reels.

"Okay, only a couple more things. After any fish strike, when an angler has the opportunity to have the fish on in the chair, the numbering system rotates one position clockwise. Number one will move to the starboard corner rod, and number six will be the starboard outrigger. Also, as the skipper has told you at the time of booking (hopefully), any fish over 100 pounds will be the property of the boat. Proceeds from the sale of fish and tips are how the deckhand is paid. If you would like to have a trophy fish mounted, the captain would be happy to help you with that. If we catch smaller fish, we will be happy to share some with you. We will give you plenty to fill your belly, but not your freezer. While we are out here we will be busily scanning for signs of birds or anything floating on the surface. If you see birds diving in the water or something bigger than a coconut floating, please let one of us know. Any other questions? Okay, let's go find some fish!"

I find the meat cleaver and chopping board and proceed to the task of preparing for the day. The cooler has three frozen five pound tuna wrapped in newspaper, one aku (skipjack tuna) and two 'ahi (yellowfin tuna). there are a couple of gallon bags of frozen opelu (mackerel scad), a five pound box of squid and about five pounds of sardines in a kitchen garbage bag. I choose two of the thirty rigged bait hooks that are hung on the cabin bulkhead behind the ladder to the flying bridge. They are 6/0 hooks with six foot 150 pound test leaders. I take the opelu and thread the point of the hook up from the lower jaw through the upper jaw. The leaders are attached to the two International 50 pound rods in the rocket launcher pole holder on the bridge, next to the center rigger 130. The slack in the leader is fastened to the ladder rail with a small wire so that it is out of the way and can be easily removed to be deployed quickly. The two baits go in the cooler on top of everything. I chop up one of the tunas and half of the anchovies into a mush with very small pieces and fill a twelve inch cylindrical bait cage from a lobster trap with the fine chum. The rest is returned to the bags and put in the bottom of the cooler. The second ahi is chopped into roughly one inch chunks and half of it goes into a two gallon plastic bucket along with several handfuls of whole sardines and a third of the squid cut in half. The third tuna is our "Charley". A 12/0 hook is run up through the lower jaw like the other baits and a very thick rubber band is twisted around the mouth below the hook to keep it closed. It is on a twelve foot 300 pound test leader. The extra bait is put back on the bottom of the cooler, the Charley on top with the chum basket, and the two baits on top for easy access. The chum basket has a six foot line attached to a cleat so that it can be tossed out quickly to create a scent trail. The two gallon bucket is wedged between the cooler and the side of the boat, behind the ladder to keep from moving in heavy seas. I flip the switch for the saltwater pump and shoot down the mess from the chum activities through the scuppers. One of my least favorite tasks is complete.

As I'm climbing up the ladder, Lee switches off the German pilot named Otto and heads into the waves coming from Molokai. The swell has risen to a solid three feet with occasional four footers and some frothy whitecaps. "White birds" is all he says. I don't see them, but Kris does. I pull out my binoculars and they come into view. First two, then six boobies and a couple of two-toned shearwaters. These birds are gliding along slowly and then suddenly changing direction, their swooping and stalling indicate that they are following a school of mahi mahi. Now they are about a hundred yards away, traveling from left to right in the trough. Our captain steers to starboard to get ahead of the school but doesn't increase speed. In another five minutes we are parallel with the birds and pulling ahead. Six silvery malolo fly out of the water simultaneously, and one is caught in the air by a boobie. The birds fly up and stall, and the skipper turns to port at a safe enough distance to keep the boat from spooking the fish while placing our lures directly in their path. A shiver runs up my spine and my hair stands at attention as a mahi lights up in brilliant colors of yellow and green and slices through a cresting wave to smash the Odagiri flying fish lure on the short outrigger.

"Hanapa'a!!! Fish on! Number five, in the chair now!"

I jump below to the deck just as the long outrigger with the flower lure breaks free and the drag turns the beautiful music of a solo into a duet.

"Number one, on the starboard fish box!"

Both fish jump several times in a dazzling display of airborne maneuvers, but they appear to be hooked solidly. Kris clears the center line while I bring the rods to our anglers. Lee is reeling in the center outrigger from Never-Never-Land.

I pass the first rod to one of the young guys and remind him "Keep the rod bent!"

Kris has stowed the first rod and is working on the starboard corner as I deliver the second rod and then retrieve the port corner lure. The fish have stopped running and are slowly being worked toward the boat.

As soon as the rods are stowed Lee yells "Put out the bait cage and throw a few chunks of chum out. And get my bait out, too!"

I flip the cooler open, untwist the wire and flip the bait out on the downwind side of the fish that is almost to the boat as Lee free spools it back behind everything.

"Throw a few more chunks of chum next to my bait; keep the flow steady. Kris, stand by with the net."

These fish are in the fifteen pound range, and extremely difficult to gaff. They don't have enough weight to provide sufficient resistance for the gaff to penetrate, and they explode when they feel the metal. The first fish is coming in, and the second is only about thirty yards out.

"Okay", I tell the angler with the furthest fish, "keep the line tight but don't pull him in yet."

I slip on my gloves and reach for the leader on the first fish. It comes in fairly easily, but it is still very challenging to coordinate the capture of a very long fish with a net hoop that is not very long. As the head is pulled over the net, the netter must lift in concert with the leader handler who must let go at the proper time so that the head of the fish can drop into the bag of the net. If tension on the leader is kept up, the length of the fish prevents it from going in. We are blessed with this one, and just as Kris lifts it over the edge, I hear an alarm clock sounding off from upstairs. The skipper has hooked one on bait.

"Number one! On the other fish box, now!" Of course, number one is reeling in the second fish that hit.

"Number two, number two! On the fish box here!"

The fisherman who caught the first mahi opens the top of his recently vacated seat and Kris sticks in the fish, net and all. Lee hands me down the pole by its tip, and I insert the rod butt into the gimbal at the end of the other box. Lee yells at Kris to get the next bait out as the second fish is coming boat side. With the first fish hopelessly tangled in the net, I flip the second one aboard and onto the side of the other fish where they provide us with an impressive drumming performance. We are able to get the fish untangled from the net and stowed just as the third fish arrives. The delicate operation is successful again,

and we have three fish in the box. It is only 7:30, and we're off to a good start.
Everyone is smiling. Today will not be a whitewash. I dump a fifty pound bag
of ice over the fish and add in five gallons of water. Then I bleed the fish by
slitting the gills on both sides so that the meat will be pure white when it is cut.
Nothing hits Lee's second bait, and the birds have dispersed, so we wash down
the blood on deck and prepare to redeploy the lures. The distance of the lures
from the boat makes a big difference in their effectiveness. They are generally
adjusted so that they slide down the face of a wave in a following sea, or pop to
the surface regularly in a head sea. The four tubes that run through the heads
of many of the lures create an impressive bubble trail-but only if they can get
above the surface to capture air.

Once everything is set to the captain's approval, he says "Grab my small foil
packet on the manifold and a passion orange drink for me."

He has some kind of a sausage and egg biscuit. Kris and I join him with our
warm Breakfast Jacks, and we enjoy our food from the flying bridge.

Lee is again the first to spot another small flock of six white birds in the
distance. They are working away from us, right to left. He turns slightly to port
and passes the action at a respectable distance, then straightens out in a way that
will have the fish swim directly into our lures. Less than a minute later, his Black
Salmon lure on the center outrigger is snapped free and the reel starts singing
its siren song.

"Number four! You're up! In the chair!"

This is one of the older gentlemen, and he handles the rod like he has done
it before. Kris and I hustle to clear the inside lines but leave the outrigger baits
out. The bait cage, opelu bait and chum line are all out.

"I see followers", the skipper says, and then puts the reel in free spool and
furiously pulls out line with his right hand with the clicker on to prevent a
backlash. He engages the clutch, and the drag sounds a distinct protest.

"Angler number three! On the port fish box!" Kris puts out the second bait,
and Lee free spools it back again. "Throw a few more chunks Kris, and then get
the net."

I leader number one in, and we have another fish aboard, Kris deftly dumps
this one in the fish box and I close the lid quickly. Fisherman number three is
the brother of one of the older guys, but he seems pretty awkward with the gear.
The second fish is getting close, and Lee is asking for another bait. He hands

down the swivel, Kris hooks it up and I toss it downwind, just as it is time to leader number two. This fish is feisty at the boat, bounding from side to side and almost jumping in the boat at one point. We finally get it netted, but the hook is caught in the net when we bring it aboard. Kris lays the net on the deck, I throw a towel over the fish's head, and it stops thrashing. I'm able to pull the hook out with pliers, grab the fish by its eye sockets and tail as Kris opens the box with one still lively fish inside, and quickly closes it after number two goes in. We manage to get the third fish in the box, but we resemble a comedy routine by not being able to net it. I finally swing it in the box by the leader, where it promptly jumps out and thrashes around the deck until I can get the towel over its eyes. At this point all six people have caught fish, a rarity on fishing charters in our harbor. Once again, the birds and fish scatter and Lee reels in his bait.

"I guess they must have taken roll call", he says.

We repeat the drill, wash down the deck, get the lures back out, bleed the fish and prepare the baits. I dump the contents of the chum basket into the bucket and refill it, and then add another half a bag of ice to the brine. If the mix is too soupy, the fish move around too much and rub against the sides of the box and each other, losing scales and their color, bringing a lower price at the fish auction. In another fifteen minutes, after the fish are stiff, we load them into the large fish box, keeping them upright with their bellies down and packing ice in between and over them. We want them to look pretty when they are delivered for sale.

"There it is, I see the buoy, and nobody's on it", Lee says. "You got everything ready on deck?"

"Aye, Captain, and it looks like there's a couple of birds hanging out there."

Kris and I clamber down the ladder and stand by. He begins his approach by making a large circle about a hundred yards away from the buoy and continues closer in concentric circles. Many times marlin or giant 'ahi hang out at a distance waiting to ambush unwary baitfish. When we are about fifty yards from the FAD, the steady drone of the diesel is silenced by four reels going off in succession. Every rod, with the exception of the longest and shortest, has a fish on.

"Jungle Rules!", I yell. "Grab a rod and keep the line tight!"

Kris reels in the short corner with the giant super plunger tuna imitation, while Lee cranks in the long center rigger. When he has the Black Salmon lure halfway back, another mahi attacks the lure, and we have five on at the same time. The strategy in this situation is simple. Everyone fights their fish from the pole holder, and we start with the closest fish first. When I can grab the leader, the angler gets out of the way safely, Kris opens the fish box, I swing it in, and she closes it quickly. No time for the net. I unhook the leader, she stows the rod, and I grab the next leader. Lather, Rinse and Repeat. All goes well, until the fourth fish, when it jumps next to the boat, and literally spits the lure out at me.

"Use the net on the last one", says a voice from above. We do, and there are four more fish on board.

"That fish that got away may have spooked the rest of the school, but we'll try baiting anyway, while we have all the lures in", says our captain. "Get Charley out."

He motors slowly toward the buoy, steering with his remote controller and we drop his bait over, put out the chum basket and pass about ten yards from the downwind side of the FAD.

"Toss a few chunks of chum", he says, and I do. A dozen trigger fish appear, and two more mahi. They follow, but don't take the bait.

"They must have been sore mouthed", Lee says. "Drop Charley back."

I attach the leader of the five pound tuna to a 130 on the downwind corner and drop it back about fifteen yards. The skipper's bait is another fifteen feet behind. When the swells eliminate the slack in the monofilament, I pull the line down sharply from the first guide to the reel. This causes the tuna to pop out of the water as if it is feeding on bait. After the third pop, a pair of mahi appear and light up in electric blue colors. The smaller one inhales the skipper's bait fish and he free spools with the clicker on for a count of five before engaging the reel. The drag sounds its protest.

I have completely lost count of who has caught what, so I shout "Number one! You're up again! In the chair!"

Lee hands the rod down, Kris gets the next bait in the water and throws some chum. I pull the tuna in and stand by to handle the leader. The second fish also swallows a bait, and we have another double. We take our time with the net and manage to get both fish in the box. In the distance, we see a boat coming toward us. It is going much faster than trolling speed. They are not going to be very happy... We clean up and set up for trolling again, and it's time for lunch. Lee has a foil pack with rice and chicken wings, and Kris and I eat our burritos washed down with Arizona Green Tea. When the skipper is done, he licks his spoon clean, wipes it off with a paper towel, and puts it back into the wooden box mounted on his dashboard.

"Eewe, Gross!" Kris says. "Don't you ever wash it?"

"Why should I, it's not dirty", he replies.

A few years later, when we attend Kris' graduation from the Air Force boot camp in San Antonio, we bring her a nicely wrapped present from Captain Lee...

Shortly after lunch we start heading back to Kewalo Basin, and Kris sees an 'Iwa bird. It is the Frigate Bird, commonly called a "high flyer". True to its name, it is gliding in tight circles a couple hundred yards off our port bow. Lee switches off the autopilot and turns the wheel. There are two boobies under the 'Iwa.

"That's a sure sign of mahi mahi" he says. As we get closer, there are four more white birds, and they are not traveling, but seem to be staying in the same area.

"Keep an eye out for a floater", Lee says. A few minutes later, we sight a partially submerged section of net in the crest of a wave. The captain zig zags us on a path so that the boat stays away from the net, but the lures pass just down current from it. Sure enough, three rods go off simultaneously.

"Number three, in the chair! Four and five fight the fish from the rod holders!" I would say that our performance on deck bore more of a resemblance to the Keystone Cops than a well- oiled machine, but we do manage to get all three fish in the box. The lures and rods are stowed, and we are set up for baiting again. As we pass the net, I pop our Charley, Kris tosses chunks of chum and Lee is dropping back his bait. We hear the magical sound of line being stripped off in free spool, followed by a moment of silence as the reel is engaged, and then the drag buzzes in pulses as a fluorescent green and yellow Mahi tail walks behind the boat.

"Number six, you're up! In the chair!" Our skipper is in fine form now, barking orders to his crew and fisherman alike as if we were hooked up for the first time.

"Get the chum basket out!, throw some chunks Kris!, Get Charley in! Where's my bait? Keep that rod bent—don't give him slack! Don't mess with the net; hand line him in! Open the box! Close the box!" With such excellent leadership, we fill the box with five more fish, and then lose one. When the last one escapes, the action dies off.

"How many do we have?", Lee asks.

"I don't know— somewhere around eighteen, I think." I reply.

"Let's clean up, get the lures back out and head for the harbor", he says. And we do. We bleed, brine and pack the fish after all the lures are in position, and go up on the bridge. The skipper is still scanning the horizon, but I am not looking for birds or floaters. I start to nod off, when the hum of the engines is interrupted by a loud snap as the line breaks free from the long outrigger, followed by a 130 pound test International screaming. There is no way to accurately describe the adrenaline rush that occurs in response to that sound. It's like a shock wave that starts at the base of my neck and travels into my brain with a pleasurable explosion of electricity.

"Hanapa'a! Number five, you're up! In the chair!" Kris and I fly down the ladder and clear the two lines closest to the rod that is hooked up. A marlin of what looks like about 150 pounds is greyhounding away from the boat. Then the line goes slack, and it is leaping out of the water towards the boat.

"Gas it, skipper!" I shout and jump on the reel to try to get the slack out. When the line begins to tighten, there is no resistance- only the weight of the Flower lure. It has been my experience that only about one in seven marlin strikes end in fish boated. This one gave everyone on the boat about sixty seconds of excitement and lived to do it again.

We are about thirty minutes from the harbor, so I find my Rockstar energy drink in preparation for what is to come. Kris and I pull lines, coil up the lure leaders and pull up the outriggers. Then she runs up the yellow mahi mahi flag. Lee expertly backs the boat into the slip, forward, back, turn, forward, back. I grab the starboard bow line with the line gaff, hook it on the cleat, do the same with the port and then attach the spring line as Kris hooks on the port stern line and pulls the boat tight to the dock. We have gotten the main thing we wanted: "back to the harbor". Our anglers are extremely happy with their experience and thank us with many compliments. One of the older men hands me a folded bill, and I thank him. It has a portrait of Benjamin Franklin on it. We offload the fish and hang them on the dock so that our fishermen can provide photographic evidence of their prowess. Then the skipper filets two of the fish for them, and one for us, as Kris and I wash down the boat. We shoot down the outside, squeegee the windows, and then move to the flying bridge. The deck is next, including emptying and cleaning the fish boxes, washing the reels and lures and hanging the rods on the ceiling of the cabin. Midway through our cleanup, the guests depart, and Kris and I help to load the rest of the fish into Lee's truck to be delivered to the auction. We finish scrubbing the back deck and Kris wipes down the seats and table while I vacuum the carpet. A once over in the head and we are done for the day. Lee gets back from his delivery and we sit down with beers for us and a juice for Kris before we head home. The older gentleman gave him a portrait of Ben as well, so I get to keep mine. We split tips equally, and I will get one third of whatever the fish go for at auction. I also get one eighth of whatever the charter fee for the day is- today he charged $600.00, so I will get $75.00. None of the other boats caught as many fish as us today, so the skipper is very happy.

"It was a good day", he says.

"Yes sir", I reply. "A day to remember."

Kenai River Sockeye Salmon Fishing- Hawaii Style

F irst published in Hawaii Fishing News July 2002
Alaska—the Great Land—conjures up images for every fisherman. Some dream of giant King Salmon screaming line from a reel, while others visualize a barn door sized halibut circling up from the depths. Still others fantasize about a 10 pound rainbow trout on a fly rod or a strong silver salmon on spinning gear.

On this, my third trip to the land of dreams, my wife and I were guests of our friends Clayton and Michelle Tanaka. We playfully dubbed them "Tanaka Tours" and made plans for a trip to the fabled Kenai River in pursuit of prized sockeye salmon. The sockeye is known in Alaska as the red salmon, for the bright red color of the flesh, and is considered by most people to be the tastiest of the five salmon species. Rounding out our group is Clayton's mom, Pat, and his brother Jason. Clayton is a surfboard blank shaper, Michelle is our church secretary, Pat runs an elementary school cafeteria, Jason is a plumber, and my wife, Annette, and I run a ceramic tile contracting business. We are six Hawaiians in Alaska attempting to catch the elusive *Oncorhyncus Nerka*.

The Kenai River is the number-one fishing destination for visitors to Alaska. It boasts strong runs of sockeye, silver, and also pink salmon in even years (like 2002). In addition, the largest sport-caught king salmon (94.7 pounds) came up from the Kenai River in 1985.

Our trip is scheduled from the fourteenth to the twenty fifth of July to coincide with the peak of the red salmon run. We caught the midnight flight from Honolulu to Anchorage, arriving at 6:00 a.m. After a hearty breakfast at Gwen's Old Alaska Restaurant (try the sourdough pancakes with reindeer sausage), we stocked up with provisions from the big box stores.

We went to Ship Creek to watch king salmon spawning, and then were off along the shores of Cook Inlet to the Kenai River. Snow-capped mountains rose from the foggy water, and the views, and temperature, were breathtaking. We stopped to watch Dall sheep frolic on the mountainside only a few miles from Anchorage. Cold, crisp, clean air burns our lungs. What a refreshing contrast to the summer heat of Honolulu!

After a three hour ride, we reach our destination in the Kenai Keys area, approximately 46 river miles up from the ocean. Clayton's friend, Bob King generously provided us with the use of his "Frontier Cabin" and boat. The cabin has a hand pump in the kitchen sink, propane and wood stoves for cooking and heating—and an outhouse. Showers are available ten miles away at the Wash Out Laundromat ($3.50 single, $5 for married couples). It can be described as suburban camping. I am in heaven.

By the time we unload the van and car, unpack and launch the boat at Dot's Fish Camp, it is 9:00 p.m. After being awake for the best part of 36 hours and traveling 1,500 miles, there was only one thing for the three men to do— go fishing! After all, we have two good hours of daylight left.

We get in the boat and motor downstream (why is the motor smoking?) to an area called "The Bluffs". Landing the boat and securing it to a deadfall, we walk upstream a few yards and begin the strange ritual known as sockeye salmon fishing. It can be viewed as an artistic ballet of motion or reduced to a lesson in applied physics. It may be seen as a function of both.

It is a well-known fact that once a sockeye enters fresh water, it stops feeding and its stomach begins to shrink. The only goal of the salmon is to swim upstream to the place of its birth, spawn and then die. There are T-shirts in Alaska with pictures of salmon emblazoned with the slogan "Spawn and Die". Although many anglers claim that a sockeye bites a fly out of instinct or irritation, it could be that we are engaged in a process of glorified snagging. Only salmon hooked in the mouth can be retained toward the three fish limit. The limit is increased to six fish when the optimal escapement goal is surpassed. Fish hooked anywhere besides the mouth must be left in the water and released as gently and quickly as possible.

Now, let's get back to the river bank and the ritual. A length of line a few feet longer than the rod is stripped off the reel, and the weighted line and fly are plopped (I can't honestly call it casting) upstream at approximately the ten o'clock position. The current carries the fly downstream, and the angler pulls the rod tip along, hoping to hook a fish on the drift. At the three o'clock position, the weight is pulled out and plopped back to the starting position.

If the ritual is performed properly and the salmon are passing through, every tenth, twentieth, or one hundredth plop will result in a fish. The hookup feels like you have hooked a rock or tree on the bottom. In fact, you may have hooked a rock or tree. If it is a sockeye, the "rock" will pull very hard, then jump once or twice and head either downstream or straight out into the middle of the river. The largest and strongest fish make it into the mainstream of the current and usually break off. This is known as a premature tag and release without the tag. Those that are foul hooked (in the back or tail) frequently make it into the main current and pull the hook free. The best technique for landing the fish seems to be to apply smooth steady pressure after stopping the initial run downstream. The urge to return to the lake is so strong that the fish will begin swimming back upstream after the first run if the pressure is slow and steady.

Back to our story. I begin the plop, drift, 2, 3, 4, 5, 6, 7, pull routine. Plop, drift, 2, 3, 4... The sonar counter at the mouth of the Kenai registered an escapement (from the hazard of the commercial nets) of ten thousand fish. This means that there are a lot of fish swimming by our position on the bank. Having no experience with this type of fishing, I mimic Clayton's technique to the best of my ability. This is his tenth trip to the river. Suddenly, I feel resistance followed by a surge of power, and then a sickening emptiness. So... there *are* fish swimming past.

A half hour later, I have a solid hookup. The fish jumps twice and then heads downstream against the smooth resistance of the drag. A few minutes later I lead its head over the net held by my friend Clay. A dime bright male of almost eight pounds lays quivering on the bank with sea lice still squirming on its scales. This is fishing! The sun begins to set, and we head back to the cabin with great expectations for this trip.

The following day we are up at 7:00 a.m. and ready for our first full day of fishing. I must admit that I knew more about catching sockeye on the first day than I did on the second. Clay caught three fish; Jason and I were tied with zero. To make matters worse, we watched at least 12 giant king salmon boated by anglers drifting by our fishing spot. The *coup de grace* came when, at the end of the day, a 50-plus pound King salmon free-jumped not twenty yards from where we stood. Three thousand plop-drift-pulls, three missed hookups, and watching several nearby anglers catch their six fish limit of sockeyes gave me a great lesson in humility on day two. Thankfully, God opposes the proud but He gives grace to the humble.

Day three found us on a quest for halibut with Alaskan Trophy Charters out of Ninilchik. Captain Don Erwin fished us hard for twelve hours.

Although we didn't get any trophies, we did catch our limit of two tasty halibut per angler.

The next day found us back on the Kenai. The sonar counted thirty thousand fish entering the river. After studying the successful fishermen near us, I increased my weight from three eighths of an ounce to three quarters of an ounce, and my leader length from three to six feet. The anglers landing fish also seemed to be speeding up the rate of their retrieve as the fly nears the bank, striking hard at any sign of resistance. The most effective fishermen also pulled the line with their left hand at the end of the retrieve, much like a fly fisherman pulls the line when false casting. This extends the amount of line cast on each plop and the amount of water covered. These modifications, and the strength of the run, result in my first limit of six fish. Clay also got his limit and Jason got on board as well.

On day five I found myself fishing next to a *cheechako* (Alaskan for greenhorn) named Norbert who manages a hardware store in Kansas. I am finally hooking fish consistently, and Annette, Michelle and Pat are also catching. Jason and Clay are pulling them in like old pros. Norbert's tenacity and lack of success are identical to my experience on day two, and he gazes at our expanding stringers of fish after each landing. He finally asked me what they were biting and looked shocked when I told him "I don't think they're biting anything; we're snagging them in the mouth."

When I had caught my limit and Norbert is still fishless, I ask him if I can tie my terminal gear on his rod in the name of a scientific experiment. Within ten minutes of tying on the weight, leader and fly, Norbert landed his first Alaskan sockeye. He offered to pay me for the tackle, but I told him to just visit Hawaii and spend lots of money. He said his wife wanted to do that anyway. The smile on his face was priceless.

Day six proves to be our most successful and humorous. We are fishing next to a professional guide who is becoming increasingly frustrated with his clients' inability to catch fish. His face keeps turning more intense shades of red. On the other side of our group, a party of four men solemnly continue the ritual of plop-drift-pull with scant results.

Annette taunted them by saying "You just have to call them like this 'here fishy, fishy, fishy', and then she hooks another, within ten feet of where they are fishing.

The final straw comes when she catches the last fish of her limit while sitting on a five gallon bucket. One of the men asked if he could kiss her to improve his poor luck. I'm not sure if he is sincere or just wants a kiss, but I told him that she is married, and the answer is "No!"

Seriously, I can tell you everything I know about sockeye salmon fishing in about 60 seconds. Reading it may take a little longer. There are two parts: equipment and technique. The most common rods and reels that we saw were spinning, although bait casting outfits are probably superior, and fly fishing gear looks like the most fun. A lightweight graphite rod of 8 to 10 feet rated for 15 to 20 pound test line is optimal. A light reel with a very smooth, sturdy drag holding 150 yards of monofilament line is adequate. The weight of the rod and reel becomes increasingly important as the day wears on. A swivel connects the main line to the leader.

The lead weight should be heavy enough to get the fly to the bottom quickly and keep it in the path of the fish. In most stretches of the Kenai, that is between three quarter to one and a quarter ounces. We found fluorocarbon leaders of 4 to 6 feet very effective. The "fly" we used was a one inch length of orange or chartreuse yarn tied to a 2/0 or 3/0 razor sharp hook as it is snelled. Some fishermen prefer commercially made silver salmon flies, or the comet or salmon egg patterns, but our experience was that the short length of yarn was just as effective. A hook sharpener should also be used to keep the point "sticky sharp", especially after hooking rocks.

The technique of the retrieve is probably the most critical factor in the fish-catching process. Ten to twelve feet of line is paid out, and the left hand pulls out and holds a portion of the line, as in fly fishing. The lead is plopped out into the river at the ten o'clock position (or two o'clock position on the opposite bank) and the line in your left hand is released allowing the weight to sink quickly. When the bottom is felt, after about one second, begin the retrieve by bringing the rod tip steadily with the current so that the lead can be felt bouncing the bottom. The rod tip should be kept just above the water for the entire sweeping retrieve. This keeps the weight on the bottom and the hook and leader in the strike zone where the fish are swimming.

The rate of retrieve begins slowly and increases in speed. At the end of the drift, jerk the rod tip sharply and pull on the line with your left hand to gain momentum for flipping the weight back upstream. Any resistance during the drift should be met with a sharp jerk and pull on the line with the left hand. This is consistent with the definition of fishing being "a jerk on one end and a bigger jerk on the other end".

Special care must be taken to assure that the line doesn't become tangled on the rod tip or reel handle while pulling, for obvious reasons. The drag should be set to allow for that first run, and the spool may have to be slowed with your hand to prevent the fish from entering the main current where many fish are lost. If the fish is allowed to make the first run without jerking or excessive resistance, it will usually begin to swim back upstream of its own accord, apparently following that strong instinctive desire to return to its spawning grounds. The fish can then be led over a net or beached on a gravel bar. It should be dispatched with a club and then bled before putting it on the stringer.

The entire process can be expressed as a simple equation if you look at it as a lesson in applied physics: Rod length + weight + reel size + weight x (line strength + stretch factor) + lead weight x (leader length + visibility) x [size of hook (sharpness + yarn color)] x rate + angle of retrieve) x number of casts x number of fish passing by = the number of fish caught. Simple enough. But then again, it may be more art than science. Perhaps that is the attraction.

If you do happen to get to the Kenai next year, keep an eye out for me and Norbert. I have a feeling that we'll both be there.

● ● ● ●

2003 My father was a hunter. I am a hunter. There is certainly an ethical and moral case that can be made for adopting a diet that does not require the death of animals, but there are no apex predators that ascribe to it. Hunting allowed our ancestors to not only survive, but also to thrive in harsh environments. It is an innate part of our being for those of us who engage in it. Ethical hunters have a great respect and appreciation for their quarry, and the life that they give sustains us in a way that is more than simple nutrition. There is an instinctive drive and emotional gratification that comes when in the outdoors, pursuing wild game. It is a part of my being. The old saw (translated as "meme" for you Gen Z'ers) is that there is a Native American Indian alternate translation of "Vegetarian". It is "Poor Hunter".

The hunting opportunities on the island of Oahu are pretty limited. There are two places that are open for public bird hunting- Ka'ena Point and Makua Kea'au. Both are wild and rugged country, very dry and desolate landscapes. Most of the birds are planted pheasants, although there are wild reproducing colonies of francolins and dove. One opening day, I hunted with our Brittany Chelsea at Ka'ena. We were next to a Fish and Game feeding and water station where the farm raised pheasants and other game birds are released. It seemed that there were hunters everywhere. A trio was walking toward us about seventy yards away, and they flushed a bird. Two shotgun blasts rang out and I was pelted with bird shot. No, it wasn't Dick Cheney. The pheasant flew away unscathed. We left Ka'ena, never to return for bird hunting.

The following weekend, my daughter Kris accompanied Chelsea and I to Makua in order to avoid the hordes and hunt wilder birds. On a windswept ridge several miles from our entry, Chelsea flushed an Erckels Francolin, the biggest species of the francolin family-about the size of a pheasant. I once asked my dad how you could tell the difference between a game bird and a song bird. He replied "If it scares the hell out of you when it takes off, it's a game bird." This one did, and by the time Kris got grandpa's old Winchester Model 12 shotgun up to her shoulder, the bird was gone. And that's why it's called hunting.

We continued hiking uphill to a saddle where the landscape had steep slopes leading from Makaha on the right to Makua on the left. The ridge trail followed the spine of the mountain in both directions. We were surprised by two goats that almost ran into us before stopping briefly and then scurrying up the trail to Pu'u Kea'au on our left. The speed and agility of the goats was amazing to see. These are feral goats that have escaped from a ranch and are now thriving in the wild. The bird hunting season follows the closing of the goat season, and our shotgun was loaded with number six bird shot, so these animals were not in any danger. Their swift departure let us know that we weren't their friends, though. Not being enamored with the bird hunting opportunities, I think we both were impressed with the possibility of going after goats the next year.

I have a tile job for a family in Mililani, and the husband is an avid bowhunter who pursues goats in the area we want to go. "You can get the goats", he says, "but you've got to really want them. They are in their sanctuary at the very top of the mountain. You will know you're in the right spot when you see an American flag. It was placed there by a Viet Nam veteran."

Kris and I make our debut as goat hunters the following year when we go with Jay Nakasone, a friend from church who has had success hunting in Makaha above his grandparents' property. Kris and I hike almost to the top where we are successful with two goats, and Jay hikes up to help us carry them down. It is exhausting work on the steep terrain-especially with the afternoon heat. And did I mention the smell? From this point forward, we will bone them in the field and reduce the weight and odor. We have more adventures with Stan Tangonan and Ren Ilog. We hunt separately but are there with walkie talkies in case anyone needs help. I have a hunt with Bryan Miyazaki, but he twists an ankle near the top and we head down early. He helped Kris to harvest a buck Axis deer on Lanai and is a very successful deer hunter. His assessment is that the terrain and difficulty are definitely not worth it for goats. After the events described in this story, I had several memorable hunts with John Reeves, when he was dating Kelly. Kelly demurred from joining us, still having disturbing flashbacks when I returned from a hunt and pulled a lamb out of my backpack. On one of these hunts, John narrowly misses a billy. I should have taken more time with him at the rifle range. On another, hunting with Stan, we came upon a herd of about ten. Stan shot one big billy while it was enamored with a nanny. The others scattered, but one goat stopped on a promontory. I hesitate to put a distance on it, but it was over 200 yards. I told Stan that I would shoot first, and he could back me up. To everyone's surprise, the goat did a full forward somersault when I shot and hit the ground in goat heaven. Stan recovered his and helped us to find ours and then went to bone his. I gutted the billy and then cut off the genitalia and threw it over the cliff.

"That's what is going to happen to you, if you ever mistreat my daughter, John."

It was a memorable hunt for all. But let's get to the story. Kris wants to bring her BFF Keli on our first adventure of the next year. I express my concern over the danger and difficulty of the hunt, but Kris assures me that she has the necessary stamina.

"She plays *soccer*, dad."

I'm also concerned because Keli is a vegetarian or vegan or pescatarian, or something in between. For a while she didn't eat anything with a face; does that mean eggs and clams are okay? Then it was no eggs or dairy, and then, inexplicably, chickens were okay. I'm concerned that she might be distressed if we do kill something. Fast forward to the Friday before the first Saturday in August—hunting is only open on weekends and holidays in August and September. It is 8:30 at night, and Kris and I are going to bed. Keli is sleeping over. All our gear is laid out and ready. I will have a Winchester Model 94 30/30 and Kris will have Grandpa's Winchester Model 70, 30/06. We have heavy socks and hunting boots, Blaze Orange shirts, Camelbak backpacks and an extra 2 liter water bottle each. We pack handheld VHF radios, PB and J sandwiches and granola bars. I have an old cotton bed sheet and my Buck pocketknife.

My alarm goes off at 3:30 am. The coffee is brewing, and we load everything in the truck. It is almost an hour drive from Mililani to Makua. As we pass the overpass at Waikele, Kris spots a miscreant tagging the pylon and calls 911 to report him. She is working and doesn't want her tax money going to erase graffiti. We pull on the side of the road at the locked gate in Makua, and I enter the combination from Fish and Game. I drive in and lock the gate behind. This is no place to leave a truck on the side of the road. We are near the ocean, and it is very humid and cold. Now it is 5:00 am, and pitch black. We have head lamps and switch them on. First Hawaiian Bank has a series of recreational cabins and a conference meeting room at the end of the road. We sign in at the hunter check in station (a mailbox on a post) and enter our license numbers into the log book. Keli is not hunting, so we put in "game bearer" in the blank space. We skirt the buildings and head toward the water tank above the cabins, then scramble uphill to the beginning of the ridge trail. The hike starts from near sea level and ends at an elevation of almost 3,000 feet. I'm shivering with the morning chill and anticipation, until the physical exertion heats me up. *"Just breathe through your nose and keep putting one foot in front of the other",* I tell myself. After about twenty minutes I say, "You guys look like you could use a little break."

I'M FIFTY YEARS OLD, and very happy to catch my breath as well. At 6:00, it is light enough to see without the headlamps, so we stow them in our packs. We have reached a bench where the landscape flattens and there is an elevated outcropping known as "Sniper Rock". It has a vista of several hundred yards in each direction. This is the tricky part of our ascent. There is a vertical climb up a twelve foot cliff to regain the ridge trail. The footholds are in crumbly rock, and there is little vegetation to assist. We make it up and take another short rest before ascending. Shortly afterwards, the sound of lambs in the distance is audible. They are close. There is no longer any discernible trail up the mountain, but the spine of the ridge leads us up, always up. Finally, we turn a corner, and the herd is visible on a mountainside about a hundred yards away.

UNFORTUNATELY, THE only way to reach them is to travel several hundred yards further up a series of steep precipices to get above them, and then another hundred yards to circle around behind them. There are two small goats grazing apart from the main flock, and they seem the easiest to target.

THE ASCENT FROM HERE looks sketchy, but doing it one step at a time, it looks possible. The way forward is daunting, to say the least, so I ask the girls to wait while I go on alone. The climb to the peak is the most challenging terrain yet. The potential danger accentuates the exhilaration of this stalk. I ascend a parapet carefully, and finally see the American flag at the top.

THE TERRAIN PLATEAUS and I circle behind and above the grazing goats on the opposite side of the ridge to avoid being seen. I peek over the edge and find myself in a perfect spot, about forty yards from them. I slide my pack off and place it in front of me as a bench rest. The goat is broadside to me, looking for danger below, and the iron sights on the cowboy rifle are set just behind the shoulder. I take a breath and slowly squeeze the trigger. At the crack of the rifle, it drops immediately, and the rest of the herd explodes toward Makaha, once again amazing us with their speed and agility on the treacherous terrain. I gut the goat and fill the cavity with grass to cool it as quickly as possible, and to reduce the weight to carry back. On the way, I drop it down the steepest sections in stages, and carefully place my feet in pockets of the crumbling rock. Twenty minutes later, I am safely back with our quarry. We skin and bone the meat and wrap it in the sheet, then stow it in the backpack.

THE ADVENTURE IS NOT over. We still have several miles to walk, including a few steep climbing sections. The sun is blazing, and we are thankful for the extra water bottles. The three of us finally descend into the flatlands before the hunter check in station, and the last two hundred yards are a dense thicket of kiawe trees with two inch thorns that are somehow always able to extract blood from our arms. This area is also a pasture for free ranging cattle. They eat the seed pods and leaves of the mesquite trees while making voluminous piles of manure as well. The area not only smells as a result, but also the population of flies is enormous. Our shirts and pants are soaked with sweat and the blistering sun is oppressive. A hundred yards from the clearing, I sit down and rest. A fly lands on one of my bloody scratches, and I dig deep to find the energy to swat it. Finally, we are rested enough to continue, and very thankful for the water jug stashed behind the seat in my truck. Then it's off to

Mickey Dees in Waianae for extra-large milkshakes all around. Organic vegan milkshakes.

MOST OF THE GOAT MEAT will be cut into strips and marinated in a teriyaki sauce and then smoked for an hour or more with mesquite. We also make traditional barbacoa tacos with minced goat. Keli hung in there throughout the entire adventure, and comported herself well when the goat was shot. They are considered an invasive species, feeding on endangered flora, and the hunting of them is regulated as such, so perhaps that is a rationalization for acceptance. The one thing that I am certain of is that the beauty of the area and the challenge of the hunt were both extraordinary, and the company was as well!

"You can get the goats, *but you gotta really want 'em...*"

Stan, Ren and John

POSTSCRIPT: IN DOING research for this story, I discovered that the property formerly owned by First Hawaiian Bank is now Our Lady of Keaʻau, a serene and scenic Franciscan retreat on 58 acres at the base of a hillside in ʻOhikilolo Valley. They minister to the large number of homeless in the area. The trail is now marked by pink ribbons, and there are ropes in the steep cliff portions. It sounds a little tame. But the goats are still wild and thriving.

Fishing With Annette

First published in Fish Alaska Magazine November 2004

It all started when I returned home to Hawaii from my second trip to Alaska. I told my wife, Annette, "I won't go again unless you come along."

Did you ever say something and then wish that you could just grab the words and stuff them back into your mouth and swallow them before the person heard? My grasping in the air was quite entertaining, but unsuccessful.

"Must've been a Yakutat mosquito from my carry-on bag", I muttered.

Early the following spring, my friend Clay Tanaka and I planned a trip to the Kenai River for mid-July with his wife Michelle, brother Jason, and mom Pat, and of course, my blushing bride, Annette. We timed our trip for mid-July at the peak of the sockeye and king salmon runs. A few other people had the same idea. I began feverishly planning for the trip of a lifetime... a side trip to Homer for halibut and ling cod, Seward for the early silver salmon in Resurrection Bay, a full day guided king salmon charter on the Kenai, another side trip to Deep Creek for halibut and maybe a few hours of clam digging at nearby Clam Gulch.

However, our primary quarry was the succulent sockeye salmon. When I divulged the scope of my plans to Annette, her response was, "You have fish gluttony; you need therapy."

I don't have fish gluttony. I like to think of myself as a serious subsistence sport fisherman. Sort of like Cheechako fish camp. We don't have salmon and halibut in Hawaii.

Before we left, Annette said, "You know, I'm not like you are... I don't mind fishing for a few hours a day, but after that, it's like, boring..."

I didn't tell her that God created twenty hours of daylight in the summer so that we can fish that long. But I am a sensitive, caring husband— I changed the king salmon charter to half a day.

It took us a couple of days to figure out how to catch the red salmon from the bank of the Kenai, but then we had a great time fishing next to the newcomers who had not quite learned the technique and terminal rig requirements. We had ten bright salmon on the stringer that our fishless neighbors kept staring at longingly when my wife told them "You just have to whistle like this, and then say 'Here, fishy, fishy, fishy...'"

The three men who were decked out in waders and fly-fishing vests gritted their teeth and looked even more serious. Annette sat down on a five-gallon bucket and caught the last of her six-fish limit. One of the men asked if he could kiss her to change his luck, but I was against the idea.

The next morning, I jumped out of bed at 4:30 without an alarm for our charter trip. Annette was somewhat less enthusiastic. At 5:45 we left the cabin to meet our guide on the ramp at Dot's Fish Camp. I was so excited that I began to walk double-time.

About then, I felt a sharp "thwack" between my shoulder blades, delivered with the admonition, "Hey, this is supposed to be a *vacation*."

We fished with a father and son from Seattle and the son caught a 63 pound king. I was blessed with a 21 inch rainbow trout. The father expounded on the sacrifices he made to fish the Kenai every year until Annette told him that he needed therapy.

He went on and on about how much better the fishing was yesterday until Annette told him, "That was yesterday, this is today. Get over it."

The guide nodded approvingly. The trip was pretty quiet after that.

When we were done fishing, we took off on the Seward Highway to Resurrection Bay, voted the most scenic road trip in Alaska. The day-trip salmon charter I had wanted was scrapped for a wonderful live Alaska King Crab dinner at the Crab Pot restaurant... I love my wife. Maybe I can catch silvers or one of those giant halibut we saw next time.

After a successful side trip (men only) to Ninilchik for halibut, and a week of red fishing, the chest freezer is beginning to fill. Annette announces, "You guys have fish gluttony. You need therapy." We men smile and look away.

On Friday my wife and I drove the 90 miles to Homer-the self-proclaimed "Halibut Capital of The World." Little does she know that I have us booked on a 12-hour combination halibut and lingcod charter. Some things are better left unsaid. We caught our limit of tasty halibut, and saw sea lions, walrus, otters, porpoises and whales. I valiantly fought and landed a twelve foot length of bull kelp as well. It may have been a new world record, but we tagged and released it. Then it was back to the Kenai for our last full day of sockeye fishing. The freezer is full, and the unavoidable pronouncement is once again made: "Gluttony/ Therapy".

Finally, we are at the hotel in Anchorage waiting for our flight home to Honolulu. Clayton's wife, Michelle, is jumping up and down on the bed with a gleeful look on her face. Clay thinks she's happy about all the fish we are bringing home. Annette smiles and looks away.

When we board the airplane for our trip home, the pilot comes on the intercom to congratulate all the fishermen on their bountiful success. He then announces that the loadmaster has determined that all baggage and cargo must be unloaded, re-weighed and reloaded to be sure that the weight distribution is correct. We are delayed for one and a half hours. The inevitable happens. Annette turns sideways, squints her eyes slightly and pronounces "I told you so... You guys have fish gluttony... You need therapy." I nod and smile. Then a thought comes to me... *THERAPY!* What a wonderful name for a boat. I love fishing with Annette.

Fishing in the *Real Alaska*

First published in Hawaii Fishing News, April 2003

"It doesn't look like we'll be able to go fishing in Alaska this year, Papa. The people we went with last year aren't going, and the other group had to cancel."

After a short pause my dad said, "I'd like to go back again. Why don't you start looking around for a good place?"

A giant smile threatened to swallow my face. We live in Hawaii, but in the summer our thoughts turn to fishing in Alaska.

My first idea was to return to the Kenai to try for King and Red Salmon during mid-July. I found a special at a Kenai lodge and showed dad a "Let's Go Fishing" segment featuring the excellent fishing.

Everything was looking good until he asked "Will we be staying in a cabin, and what will we eat?"

"Well dad, we'll be staying at the Trophy Lodge, which is kind of like a big hotel, and we can eat at the restaurants in Soldotna. There's even a Taco Bell and McDonald's."

The Kenai is a suburban wilderness that combines wild moose strolling through the neighborhood and strong salmon runs with a Fred Meyer superstore that is as big as our Safeway and Wal-Mart combined.

Dad said, "McDonald's and Taco Bell... *that's* not the *Real Alaska!*" Back to square one.

I had been intrigued by Joe Upton's book, Alaska Blues, which is his story of one season of commercial fishing in Southeast Alaska. He spent most of his time at a remote cabin on the northern tip of Prince of Wales (POW) Island. The book Fishing Alaska by Limeres and Pedersen also gave excellent reports of the fishing on the west coast of POW. Prince of Wales is the third largest island in America, after the Big Island of Hawaii and Kodiak Island. The population is 4,886 on an island 45 miles wide and 135 miles long. Internet sites confirmed that this area has some of the best fishing in the world. Unfortunately, many of the POW lodges are in the thousand dollar a day range. Dad and I are Scotsmen at heart, and besides, all that pampering didn't seem like the "*Real Alaska*".

After hours of internet surfing, I found Art and Claire King and Naukati Cabins. Claire assured me on the phone that they could arrange both skiff rentals and full day charters on a larger boat with an experienced skipper. They had an opening for us at the end of July and beginning of August. I was encouraged that Naukati wasn't listed in the 2002 edition of <u>The Alaska Wilderness Milepost Book of Remote Communities</u>.

Our quarry of choice included feisty silver salmon in salt water and prized halibut. Thousands of fish pass through these waters at this time of year, feeding on the abundance of bait on their way to their spawning grounds. The salmon spawn in their natal rivers, and the halibut migrate to deeper waters in the Gulf of Alaska where they spawn in January.

Art King promised, "You're gonna love the fishing here!" and he was right.

Naukati is a small village (population 135) on the northwest side of POW Island. The primary jobs are logging and fishing, both of which have been hit pretty hard. Logging on public lands, the Tongass National Forest, was curtailed by the Clinton administration, and the prices for salmon have plummeted (37 cents for sockeye) as a result of the glut of farmed Atlantic salmon on the market.

Dad and I recruited my brother-in-law Gene Barham from Florida to join us and finalized our plans. We scheduled four days of skiff fishing and three days of charters with Capain Greg Richter on his 26' Olympic.

On the 27th of July, Dad and I flew from Honolulu to Seattle, and then on to Ketchikan, where we met Gene. Early the next morning, we were at ProMech Air admiring a mounted 50 pound king salmon in their waiting room and preparing to board a twin engine Otter floatplane to take us to Thorne Bay. We were dazzled by the spectacular scenery on the flight. Emerald green forested mountains rise sharply from the cobalt water. Snow-capped granite peaks kiss puffy cumulus clouds in the pale blue sky. The air is crisp, clean and exhilarating.

Art had delivered a Chevy Suburban for us to drive the 44 miles from Thorne Bay to our final destination of Naukati. Prince of Wales Island has over 1,000 miles of logging roads, mostly gravel, and the scenery is spectacular. We saw several bald eagles and eight Sitka black-tailed deer. Arriving in Naukati, we met Art and Claire and were extremely pleased with our cabin. The exterior was rustic wood, and the interior very clean and comfortable. Captain Greg was waiting for us. We were scheduled for a short day charter to orient ourselves and scout the areas we could fish from the skiffs on our own. We stowed our gear and made a quick stop at the Naukati Connection. The Connection is the only store in the community, and it has everything from boats and motors (including rentals) to food, hardware and dry goods. The prices are about what you would expect for such a remote area.

Then we were off to the floating dock at Little Naukati and our first fishing adventure. Captain Greg had his Olympic gassed and ready to go. We headed out past two channel markers and turned into Skookum Chuck. *Skookum* is a native word for swiftly moving waters. Thousands of gallons of water flow through this pass during a fifteen foot tide change. Soon we were far from Naukati, headed for Port Alice, one of Captain Greg's favorite spots. We begin "mooching" for silver salmon with level wind reels and limber seven foot rods. We attach a two to six ounce keel sinker to the main line with a swivel. A four to six foot length of twenty to thirty pound test mono with a sliding two hook rig is used to bait a "plug cut" six inch herring. The herring is cut at a compound angle behind the head and pierced with the first hook "in at ten, out at two" while the trailer hook is imbedded in the narrow part of the tail. The sliding hook is tightened to bend the bait slightly. The curve in the bait and the blunt front combine to cause the bait to spin seductively through the water. Within minutes of starting to fish, Gene has a ferocious strike. His rod doubles over and the fish screams out 100 yards of line in an incredibly strong first run.

"You've got a king on!" our skipper shouts with glee. After half an hour and several more powerful runs, Gene brings a huge salmon to the net.

"ISN'T GOD GOOD WITH the gifts He gives us?" he says.

"Yes, He is, Henry Eugene, yes He is. . ." Such a Blessing. Our first fish weighs 54 pounds at the dock. What a way to start the trip!

Dad was mooching his rig shortly after when his rod bent sharply and a ten pound silver salmon jumped one, two, three and four times. It slashed back and forth strongly and then came to the boat where it made a last run before Greg gaffed and swung it aboard in one smooth motion. We continued mooching for three more silvers and then Greg showed us his method for trolling.

The rigs consist of a weight between 4 and 16 ounces attached to a flasher and a 2 to 4 foot leader with either a hoochie or a herring bait. The flasher is a metal or plastic plate about 4 by 12 inches long that runs through the water in an erratic dodging path, reflecting light like a feeding fish or bait school. Popular colors are silver, green and pink. The hoochie is a 4 inch octopus skirt; pink and white, black and silver and green and silver are popular choices. The hoochie can be sweetened with a quarter of a herring filet pinned to the hook as a "sniffer". Diving planers like the Dipsy Diver or Pink Lady can be used in lieu of weights to get the bait down. We trolled by Gas Rock and Big Sandy Beach with a commercial troller for six more silvers and a big pink salmon, and ended the day extremely tired and happy. The next two days will be self-guided.

EARLY THE NEXT MORNING we went to the Naukati Connection to get our Hewescraft fishing boat. Unfortunately, a local lodge had a problem with their own boat and hadn't returned the boat when they were supposed to. After losing half a day, we ended up with two 16 foot Lund skiffs at no cost except extra gas (Thanks, Andy) and charged out to Sea Otter Sound, bound for Big Sandy Beach and Port Alice. The afternoon chop sent us back to the sheltered waters. Alaska is a huge place, worthy of the utmost respect. It appears

even larger from a small skiff. We trolled around the sheltered waters and Gene
found silvers off a slough on the side of Cap Island. He caught three and lost a
few, reporting that it was like a fire drill to drive the boat and try to fight and net
the fish single-handedly. Dad and I caught one and lost two when the twenty
pound leaders broke. Our third day was pretty discouraging. We opted to use
one skiff. I fished the morning with dad and the afternoon with Gene. Dad and
I tried for silvers where they were the day before, but nobody was home. We
drifted and bottom fished for a few small rockfish but found no halibut. The
afternoon with Gene wasn't much better. We hope for better action the next
day with Greg.

We were told that the silvers stay in the outside waters feeding until the
rains come. When the streams rise they come into the sheltered waters and
coves, searching for their natal streams. The pink salmon come to spawn in the
lower reaches of the streams and in the estuaries. Halibut come to feed on the
spawned-out salmon carcasses. Unfortunately for us, without rain this wouldn't
happen until the end of August and through September.

Our fourth day of fishing was truly incredible. Captain Greg blasted through
the maze of islands at 34 knots with his 200 Yamaha and had us fishing at
Black Rock in Warren Channel in less than an hour. When I had talked to him
in April, I asked if he did salmon and halibut combination trips. He replied,
"First we'll go out and slay our limit of salmon, and then we'll go pick through
the halibut to get a limit of decent fish." I wanted to believe him, but my
experience has been that most things that seem too good to be true aren't. This
day was an exception to the rule. We fished in proximity to the "thousand
dollar a day lodge" boats. Mooching next to bait balls, we had our limit of 18
silver salmon by noon. Then we headed out across the channel to Warren Cove
for halibut. We caught a thirty pounder on the first drop, and three more
keepers in the next two hours. Greg called it "slow" and then moved to a place
he called "The V" to catch two more for our limit. Unbelievable! On the way
back to port, we decided to scrap the last two days of self-guided fishing in
favor of going out with Greg.

BACK AT THE DOCK, I filleted the salmon while Greg cut the halibut. His niece Vanessa and wife Carin came to help us skin and bag the catch. The freezer was filling up, so we sent three seventy pound boxes out with the mail plane for ProMech Air to store for us in their walk-in freezer.

Day five was almost as good, but the weather was so clear, warm and bright that the salmon were playing hard to get. By noon there were five fat silvers in the box and we opted to look for halibut. Greg uses a standard Alaska halibut rig with a metal spreader bar, a sixteen ounce cannonball sinker and a leader with either J or circle hooks. I brought bottom fishing rigs with quality Japanese three-way swivels, 80 pound Mason hard monofilament and #36 Maruto hooks. Drifting during the slack water at the tide change, we dropped our baits to the bottom in water from one hundred to two hundred and fifty feet deep. Pull up a crank, and then tap-tap-tap until you get a bite. The halibut usually mouth the bait to get a taste before they get serious about eating it. The larger ones really thump the rod and pull line on the initial run.

Greg seemed disappointed that we hadn't caught one over a hundred pounds, and said they are fairly common in some years. Dad caught a huge skate that we thought was a "barn door halibut", and afterwards said that he preferred salmon fishing.

Every night at the cabin we threw a salmon or halibut filet (or both) on the BBQ. There's nothing like the flavor of freshly caught grilled Alaska fish. We also caught a variety of rockfish but threw all but one of them back. Quillback, dusky, China and copper rockfish were everywhere, but we were exhausted from cleaning all the other fish, and the size of the filets relative to the size of the fish was small. The one we did grill was excellent. It tasted like the shrimp it feeds on.Day six was another wonderful adventure. Captain Greg picked us up at the cabin and we left the dock shortly after seven. Fishing was a little less spectacular in the beginning, with four silvers and two pinks in two hours. Then it was dad's turn for some real excitement. He hooked into a freight train on his new salmon rod with 17 pound test line. A "feeder" king salmon came in and inhaled his herring. The first run showed 257 feet of line was out on his gold reel's line counter. Dad is 84 years old, but when I asked him if he wanted any help fighting the fish, he looked fifty years younger. There was a tense moment when the line caught on the transducer mount, but Greg freed it, and after about twenty minutes he netted the 42 pound trophy and whooped with joy. Halibut fishing at Warren Cove afterwards produced a 68 pounder for Gene. (Why does he always catch the biggest?) We finished our limits in Sumner Strait and were back in the harbor by 5 o'clock. That night we were treated to a special dinner of Carin's beer-battered halibut. Delicious!

OUR LAST FISHING DAY dawned foggy and wet, more like typical Southeast Alaska weather. Greg threaded his way through the maze of islands with one hundred foot visibility on radar and GPS. "Trust your GPS" was his mantra. Some of the passes between islands are less than 100 feet wide. At Port Alice, the bite was slow until we switched from 30 pound test mooching rigs to 20 lb. Then we had non-stop action with silvers. The lighter line is less visible in the clear water and gave the herring a more enticing spin. Double and triple hookups of leaping and slashing salmon were not uncommon. The excitement of the initial bite and run of these fish on light tackle is almost indescribable. Silver salmon in salt water are an adventure that will never be forgotten. We were satisfied with 16 fish, then headed to "Stu's Hole" in Sumner Strait for halibut. We got one keeper, but the current was so strong that we headed to "The V" to finish our limit. Greg wanted to toss back our last fish and try one more spot for a hundred pounder, but we were tired and more than happy with our catch.

We joked in a Scottish brogue: "You have to stay and catch your limit with Captain Greg. It costs extra to go home early, lad. Cut some fresh bait and make another drop!" We were getting giddy. Back at the dock, Greg's family helped us process our catch and the bounty of quality filets was carefully placed in the freezer. We were completely exhausted and totally fulfilled- the two hallmarks of a perfect adventure.

THE NEXT DAY WE BID *Aloha* to the Kings and Greg and headed back to Thorne Bay for the floatplane ride to Ketchikan. Early the next morning we caught Alaska Air to Seattle and said goodbye to Gene. It was great to fish with him again. Maybe next time he'll let me catch the biggest fish. Dad and I made it back to Honolulu with six fish boxes and one cooler of salmon and halibut- more than 400 pounds of first-quality filets. The next few days were devoted to smoking and vacuum packing our catch. we gave away a lot, but froze enough for the winter and spring months. Every time I pull a package from the freezer, I remember that adventure with Gene and dad, fishing in the *Real Alaska*!

Señoritas Fishing Tournament

First published in Hawaii Fishing News June 2004

F

ON THE SECOND DAY OF the Hawaii Yacht Club Senoritas Fishing Tournament, we were a little more than halfway across the Molokai Channel, headed for P Buoy. The twin diesel engines on the *Sea Verse III* were droning along steadily when we heard an unmistakable "Zzzt,zzzt" from the back deck.

"Which one was it?" I asked as I scurried down from the flying bridge.

Captain Lee said "I think it was the port corner. Might be a marlin."

I dropped back the lure, and then cranked it back quickly-drop back, crank. I felt a heavy weight, and the reel started to give line. As quickly as it started, the weight was gone. I continued trying to tease the fish into striking and then started to reel the lure in to check for damage.

"Leave it out for a while", Lee said. "Sometimes they follow and strike again."

I dropped it back into position on the face of a wave where the jets can scoop air creating an enticing bubble trail. After five minutes I cranked the lure in and found the line ahead of the lure scratched from a marlin's bill.

"Definitely a marlin", I told Lee. "but not bad enough to change the leader."

As I was dropping the lure back into position, the starboard outrigger clip snapped, and the reel screamed in protest as line was released from the spool.

"*Hana Pa'a!*, Outrigger!" I yelled, as if nobody else had noticed.

I pinched the inside of the reel spool to insure that the hook was set. This time we wouldn't have to tease the marlin. The billfish broke the surface about 75 yards away and thrashed the surface with its bill. It looked to be about 200 pounds, although I couldn't dance down the wake with my digital scale.

"I told you they follow sometimes", Lee said from the controls.

He was right. Pam Freed was in the chair, and I took the rod and slipped its butt into the gimbal. The fighting vest was put on, hooked to the reel and adjusted. Line continued to peel from the reel as the other rods were brought in and stowed.

The flying gaff was tied to the base of the chair, the second big gaff was readied, gloves put on and a pair was sent up to the captain. The fish door was opened. This Pacific blue marlin was giving Pam a hard time, but she was gamely retrieving line. It seems that marlin in the 150 to 250 pound range sometimes fight much harder than the larger ones.

After about twenty minutes, the line became slack— too slack. Lee gunned the engines, but the rod didn't bend. The hook had come out. It was nobody's fault, but the disappointment was thick. The good part was that we still had six more hours until "stop fishing" at four o'clock. And we had done very well on our drill.

This was the 25th anniversary of the two day Hawaii Yacht Club Senoritas Fishing Tournament. The entry fee was $350 per boat, and the tournament paid out cash prizes for the five heaviest fish brought in. In addition, over $5,000 in merchandise prizes were donated by over 60 sponsors. Aku, ono, mahimahi, 'ahi, spearfish and both striped and Pacific blue marlin counted, if they were above minimum weights. "Start Fishing" was at 7:00 a.m. (we got to sleep in), and stop fishing was at 4:00 p.m. The boat had to be back in Ala Wai Harbor by 7:00 p.m. to weigh fish. Twenty four teams were entered in this year's contest. The tournament was a great success as the result of the work of the volunteers.

We had won the 2003 Senoritas Tournament with a striped marlin that weighed less than a hundred pounds and was caught on the second day of the tournament. Bruce Matson, on the *Cormorant* had raised the bar this year when he brought a 196.5 pound Pacific Blue Marlin to the scales before 10:00 a.m. on the first day. No stripers were going to win this year.

Back on the boat, we were coming up on P-buoy, a FAD (fish aggregation device) near the tip of the Penguin Banks. No other boats were in sight. A mahi mahi slammed the starboard corner rod, and a smaller one grabbed the aku lure on the center rod as the line was being brought in. Both were in the boat quickly, and we were pleased to have fish in the box. We "Got the Stink Out".

We headed out to one of Captain Lee's secret spots. I have been fishing with Lee Severs for more than 18 years on the *Sea Verse I, II* and *III*. He has proven himself to be an extremely talented and successful fisherman. Nobody tries harder to catch fish for his customers, and Captain Lee is probably the best skipper in the harbor for catching mahi mahi. Then again, I may be prejudiced. I started chartering with Lee and progressed to becoming a part-time deckhand when he needed someone, and my work schedule permitted. It's been my pleasure to fish with him, especially in tournaments, and it's a bonus to get paid.

No strikes came from the secret area, so we headed back into the Molokai Channel. At 12:07, the port corner rod slammed down violently, and line was burning off the reel at an alarming rate. The drag was set fairly loose, so I pushed it up a little past the stop on the Shimano 130. I was thankful the lure was on the big reel. Sharon Attwood was up, and she was in the fighting chair, ready to reel. I slipped the rod into the gimbal, but she could only watch as line continued to melt off the spool. The entire team moved as one to clear lines and stow the rods out of the way. The fish erupted in a huge mass of white water about 400 yards behind the boat. I didn't get a good look at it, but the amount of spray told us this fish was bigger than the one we had lost. Finally, the fish slowed, and the line began to come in. Sharon did a masterful job of pulling up on the rod with the fighting vest and then smoothly reeling on the way down, maintaining steady pressure on the fish. She was a natural, and experienced. Captain Lee said it is all technique, not brute strength, and he was right again.

Lee had instructed my daughter Kris on the controls for the twin diesels so she could drive the boat when he came down to gaff.

"If there is a danger of the fish going into the prop, I'll give you the command to punch the throttle. If I give you the command, make sure you punch it. We don't want the fish to be disqualified from a prop cut."

Half of the reel's spool was full, then three quarters. I wet my leather gloves to make them more pliable. The preparations were made: flying gaff, second gaff, door open and the mallet for the coup de grace. It was very quiet on the boat.

"We've got color", Lee said from the bridge.

Next came the 300 pound test leader and the moment of truth. *Should I have cut off the chafed line? Did I crimp that sleeve well enough?* The skipper came down from the bridge and grabbed the flying gaff. I reached for the leader and felt the full weight of the fish. It was twenty feet behind and below us, shimmering silver and blue. The great fish was tired. It came to the boat like the gift that it was. Lee sank the flying gaff in the front of the hump.

"Grab the bill," Lee instructed me, and as I did, he used the mallet.

The fish lit up in an incredible display of neon blue and silver, and then it was over. It was 12:38. I set the second gaff at the back of the gill. Sharon's husband, Leon, helped Lee and me slide the fish through the door. It was time for my part of the tradition established whenever we catch a big fish.

"Praise the Lord!", I yelled loudly.

Captain Lee agreed. I iced the fish on the deck and wrapped it in a tarp for the ride back to the harbor. Lee called in the catch and conservatively estimated the weight at 210 pounds. Everyone on the boat was happy and tired.

We caught another mahimahi on the starboard corner on an Art Kamisugi lure, on the way home. Art's special lure on the long 'rigger had caught three of our four fish on the first day of the tournament. Maybe Lee will let me run one of my lures on an outrigger in the next tournament. I was happy to have had one on the port corner. If you want help with lures, go to see my friend Sonny at Pacific Ocean Producers. He's the man.

On the way back to the harbor, Lee pointed out a shearwater skimming across the wave tops to Kris.

"Do you know how to tell a traveling bird from ones that are looking at fish?"

"No. How?" Kris replied.

Lee smiled as he said, "If you look real closely, you can see tiny suitcases under their wings."

Another mahi mahi struck the same lure but shook free after five energetic jumps. "*mahi*" in the Hawaiian language means athletic. It is repeated for emphasis. "mahi mahi" means "very athletic". This fish was a long-distance tag and release without the tag. We don't have to catch them all.

Back at the Ala Wai Harbor, we bantered with the team from the *Alakazam* as we waited behind the *Blue Diamond* to weigh our fish. The *Alakazam*'s fish was 210 pounds, and they were very anxious to see ours. The *Blue Diamond*'s marlin weighed a respectable 187.5 pounds. Finally, we got our fish up on the scales, and the digital readout showed 264 pounds. What a thrill! We were winners two times in a row!

At the awards dinner the next night, Bob McCowan from the *Blue Nun* told me "You guys were just lucky, that's all."

I responded, "Maybe you could say that if it was just one year, but we won twice!"

After I said it, I felt really bad. Sorry, Bob. We weren't lucky, we were blessed. Twice! God opposes the proud, but He gives grace to the humble.

There was a bittersweet tale from this tournament, also. The *Monkey Biz* fished in the tournament on Saturday but opted out on Sunday to take a paying charter instead. They hooked up and caught a 740 pound marlin. The *Blue Nun* caught an 848 pound blue on the 30th of April, within a week of the tournament. A relatively new charter skipper, Keoni on the *Sudden Rush* has caught marlin weighing more than 500 pounds during the last two months. Everybody wants to know what he is doing. The *Magic* also caught four pacific blues on March 19, and two days later got one weighing more than 500 pounds.

You can also be a part of the charter boat fishing in Kewalo Basin, and you might even catch the fish of a lifetime!

2006 "Naukati!? Why would you want to go to Naukati!? The disenfranchised of the world flock to Naukati!", he blustered.

Quickly, a cloud of concern blew across his face.

"You aren't going to quote me on that, are you? I'll probably get visited by a vigilante committee if you do."

"We're going for the fishing— mostly", I responded, trying to conceal my surprise at his unexpected outburst.

Naukati is the centerpiece of this, my seventh trip to The Great Land.

My first trip to Alaska from Hawaii, that began this long-distance love affair, was in 1989. Dad, who lived right down the road, and my sister and brother-in-law, Kathy and Gene Barham from Florida, converged on Thorne Bay at McFarland's Floatel on Prince of Wales Island a short 40 miles west of Ketchikan. We came in by float plane and stayed in the just-finished cabins, fishing with Jim on the *Jeannie M* for 2 days, and self-guided in skiffs for 5 other days. On the first day we caught a limit of pink salmon with Jim, and Jeannie smoked them up fresh for us in a "refrigerator smoker." The air was fresh and clean, the trees were bright and green, and we even had two days of blue skies. What was not to love?

Jeannie's "Seafood Spread" dinner was a highlight of the trip. The table and floor were "spread" with newspaper and we were served an incredible feast, including sautéed sea cucumbers-delectable, baked halibut, Dungeness and tanner crab that we helped catch, and an entire bucket of butter clams. We ate and laughed until we hurt! Our experience with self-guided fishing yielded lots of rockfish, a few pink and silver salmon and a small halibut.

As Jeannie is wont to say, "The fishing was great, but the catching left a little to be desired."

My next trip with dad was to Yakutat (200 miles from anywhere) where I caught my first king salmon and lots of halibut. Then three pilgrimages were to the mecca of the Kenai River, mostly hooking reds with experienced friends, including side trips to Seward and Homer. I got my hundred pound halibut (59 pounds of filets) on an overnight trip with Alaska Coastal Marine off the Barren Islands at 2 a.m., Captains Josh and Chris attending. The Kenai Peninsula is a magical place, but it is *not* the Alaska of most people's imaginations. It's a suburban wilderness- mixing superstores and fast-food franchises with renegade moose and incredible salmon runs.

The last trip with my father was to The *Real Alaska*. I read Joe Upton's book Alaska Blues describing one season of commercial fishing in Southeast and his cabin at Point Baker on the northern tip of Prince of Wales Island (POW). Then I read Peter Jenkins' Looking For Alaska and his tale of flying into Klawock from Seward, fishing with native Haida out of Craig.

I called the ADFG fisheries biologist for POW and asked him, "Where is the best fishing?"

"Try the west side of the island", was his terse reply.

Countless hours on the internet turned up Art and Claire King's Naukati Cabins. I was encouraged that Naukati was not then listed in the Alaska Wilderness Guide. The less tourists the better.

Art assured me "You're gonna love the fishing up here!"

If anyone was more enthusiastic than Art, it was Captain Greg Richter.

"First we'll go out and slay our limit of Silvers at Black Rock, and then we'll pick through the halibut to get a limit of decent fish."

Most things that seem too good to be true aren't, but this was an exception. On the first day of our trip, my *blessed* (pick your pronunciation and meaning) brother-in-law Gene hooked and landed a 54 pound king salmon. It was a foreshadowing of things to come with near limits of feisty silvers and tasty halibut for the three of us every day and a bonus 42 pound king for my 84 year old father. He literally jumped into Greg's boat the next day. We lost my dad a few years later, but he always talked about returning to Alaska "one more time."

In 2005, my sixth trip was back to the Kenai. We arrived on the 19th of July, and on that day, the limit for sockeye was raised from 3 to 6 fish. The 4 of us had cheechako fish camp for 10 days and brought back 11 boxes of prime red filets that were carefully smoked and distributed to family and friends. As soon as the fish were processed, I began planning my seventh trip. Such is the nature of the Great Land's call.

Seven is known as the number of completion or perfection, and I wanted this trip to include my family and to be very special. Well, not the whole family, our oldest daughter Shannon got married, and was privileged to watch our other family member, a Springer Spaniel princess named Hailey. My middle daughter, Kris, will meet us at the halfway point. She joined the Air Force and was completing her training as an air traffic controller at Eielson AFB in Fairbanks. She is an Alaskan resident— something about the absence of state income taxes and the presence of the Permanent Fund. My youngest daughter, Princess Kelly, and Queen Annette (my blushing bride) round out the crew. In a rare flash of brilliance, I decided that what I *most want to do* is to return to Prince of Wales and *see the whole island.* Annette agrees but reminds me that she has concerns about the bears.

"We probably won't see any, dear", is my response...

August 1st finds us on the redeye flight from Honolulu to Seattle, and then the early bird into Ketchikan. After checking in at The Landing Hotel we catch the shuttle to Wally World for our fishing licenses. I score three 7 foot spinning rods for $8.63 each (was that the right price?) and buy Annette some Xtra Tufs. Everyone has Southeast Sneakers now-we don't have to *look* like tenderfeet. I stock up on Vibrax spinners for river fishing and then it's back to the hotel for a halibut BLT and a nap. We wake up a little groggy, but game, and catch the shuttle downtown to do the tourist thing. Fortunately, the last of 3 cruise ships is just pulling out. I gawk at people catching pink and chum salmon in the midst of heavy traffic on the bridge in the center of town. We take photos with the totem poles and make the obligatory trip to Dolly's House, "where the fish and the fishermen go upstream to spawn." Our last stop is at The Silver Lining to pick up 6 styrofoam insulated fish boxes. It's a long way home to Hawaii, and we want our valuable fish to arrive solidly frozen.

The next morning, we eat an Alaska sized breakfast and catch the 10:45 departure of the inter-island ferry *Prince of Wales.* Turning into Clarence Strait, we pass the fourth cruise ship headed for Ketchikan. With the tourist population hovering at 6,000, and climbing, it's a good day to be headed somewhere else. Onboard the ferry, we meet Sal Williams, a former POW resident on his way back to see a granddaughter who is visiting from Seattle. He drives a cab in Ketchikan but hopes to move back next year to start a restaurant.

"A bowling alley and bars is all Ketchikan has, but there's always something good to do on the island."

He talks about subsistence netting sockeye at the mouth of the Klawock River with family, and hunting for deer later in the season when they have more fat. Obviously of native heritage, his engaging smile and wry sense of humor are winsome.

"I've got to move back", he concludes.

The ladies working the Dockside Cafe grill on board want to know why we would leave Hawaii.

"To fish", my wife responds.

"Don't they have fish in Hawaii?" one asks.

"Not salmon and halibut", I tell her. What I fail to say is that we don't have "sustainable harvest" management policies like Alaska. What we do have is "*over* harvest". The near shore fishery has been nearly decimated by gill netting and the longline boats who wiped out all the swordfish in the Gulf of Mexico, are now busy working on our 'ahi (yellowfin tuna) and marlin. I rarely shore cast any more, and when I work part time as a deck hand on a six pack charter boat we have some days that are whitewashes—no fish at all, just a hot boat ride. The overcrowding and traffic congestion on my island of Oahu are rapidly making it a good place to be from. We have bumper stickers that say, "If it's tourist season, why can't we shoot them?" In contrast, almost everyone I ask about living on POW says that they really like it.

The older woman at the grill concludes "We have everything we need, and we love living here... but it does rain a lot."

Kasaan looms into sight as we near the end of our ferry ride, and we glide into Hollis on schedule, 3 hours from Ketchikan. At the ferry landing, a woman is holding a cardboard placard with my name on it (visions of greeters at Honolulu airport cross my mind, but she doesn't have a flower lei). She has brought our black Yukon rental the 42 miles from Craig to catch the ferry to Ketchikan. We drive back to Shaub-Ellison Rentals/ Gas Station/ Repair Shop to check in with Bob- the manager. My wife and daughter agree that he is a spitting image of the actor George Clooney.

"She saved you $30 on the shuttle charge", he says with a signature crooked little Clooney grin.

We ask him about fishing in the Klawock River, and he gives us directions to a spot he fished with his kids the night before.

"It's still early in the season, but there's a few silvers coming through."

Then it's off to the Trophy Inn in Klawock where we will be staying four nights. We are greeted by a giant dog appropriately named Griz. A note on the door says "Please help yourself in. We went hunting overnight." After stowing our gear, we head off to the IGA to stock up on provisions and are pleasantly surprised by the selection and reasonable prices. $107 later we are putting away food and rigging our spinning rods.

Bungling Bob's directions, we still manage to find a path that leads down to the river. The main trail is being improved as a community project by the youth. They chain saw deadfalls, build short boardwalks through boggy spots and lay down sawdust on the existing path. Within a hundred yards we answer the proverbial question of what bears do in the woods. My wife Annette is aghast staring at the impressively large pile of scat.

"What *is* that stuff?! I *told* you I don't do bears." Armed with two fishing poles and a video camera we hesitantly push on looking for a fishable spot. Finding a marginal hole in the trees the girls practice their casting skills. I hook a pink salmon which promptly swims on the wrong side of a sunken tree. As I hoist it into the air it shakes free.

After lunch we take the POW Hatchery tour. Starting at the weir which guides the fish into the sorting pool, our guide Charley (good name) points out a small black bear directly across the river.

Annette asks about how dangerous they are, and he responds, "They're hardly ever a problem."

It's the "hardly ever" that bothers her. After the tour we ask if he knows a good fishing spot and he says that the area 300 feet downstream from the hatchery (where legal fishing begins) is a popular spot. We thank him and decide to try. Our main goal seems to be to decorate the trees and river bottom with a dazzling display of #5 Vibrax spinners in brilliant colors. The rocks seem to prefer chartreuse, but the trees favor being festooned with pink and blue. We hook and lose a number of pinks, but late in the day I make a decent cast slightly upstream, and as the blades begin to flutter, a jolting strike makes all those other casts worthwhile. It's a bright silver that jumps three times and slashes upstream and then down. It flirts with a sunken tree and finally comes in where I try to smoothly slide it up onto the shore.

"Yay!" we all shout in unison; fresh salmon for dinner.

THEN IT'S BACK TO THE Trophy Inn. Don's family's hunt yields two bucks, and they generously share a roast with us (even offering the backstrap) which I slice thinly and marinate in my homemade teriyaki sauce. They process meat until the wee hours. Don and Teresa Busse's accommodations are only exceeded by their genuine hospitality. Each morning Teresa left freshly baked goodies on the shelf outside our door. The wild blueberry pie was my favorite.

The next morning it's off to Hydaburg. I want to see as much of the island as possible, and this is where a large population of native Haida live. We cruise town and then stop at the store to look for a bathroom for the women. "No Public Restroom" the sign behind the cash register reads ominously, but the friendly cashier says that we can use it anyway. The women much relieved, we continue on and find teenagers snagging pink salmon with hand lines from a bridge over the creek. A glistening fish flops over the rail and is added to a bucket with 6 spotted tails sticking out. We stop at the Totem Park next to the school and admire the forest of carved poles, ending up at the harbor and then backtracking through town.

On the way back to the main highway we stop at the Harris River where there are hundreds of pink and chum salmon clearly visible. They don't bite, but the white sox do. My first experience with them. They leave a stinging welt with a tiny drop of blood. We decide to return to the Klawock River again after lunch. The clerk at the Black Bear Store is happy to see us.

"Did you lose all those lures already?", she asks cheerfully.

"We're here to boost the local economy", Annette replies.

I also buy a serious looking can of bear spray. If "hardly ever" happens, at least we have an option other than laying on the ground and covering our heads. We venture out to find the spot marked on Bob's map and discover a nice pool with lots of elongated shadows. This must be the place, because 150 yards upstream a bear is ambling toward us. On her second cast, my daughter Kelly shouts with glee as her rod arcs and line hisses from the reel. She lands a 4 pound mouth-hooked Pink which is her first salmon. Attempting to catch the whole scene on video, I pan from the bear to Kelly with the salmon on her hook. She is very much concerned with its disposition.

"Are we gonna keep it, Dad?", she asks.

Already starting to discolor and develop a hump, we let it go. When the bear reaches a point 50 yards downstream we decide it's time to go. Discretion *is* the better part of valor...

• • • •

BACK AT THE FLAT ROCK below the hatchery, Annette smiles broadly when a fat silver solidly nails her chartreuse Vibrax. Using her smooth fighting technique, honed catching reds on the Kenai, she carefully lands it with the thin 10 pound test line. A short time later Kelly experiences the power and acrobatic jumps of a fresh chrome beauty as she lands a solid eight pounder. During the hatchery tour we learned that only fifty two silvers have made it up to the sorting pool so far this year. We are truly blessed to catch three so early in the season. We have a full day charter with Captain Lonnie Walters scheduled for Sunday, so after we finish highlighting the landscape with a few more bright points of vibrant Vibrax colors, it's off to the South Harbor in Craig to meet the skipper and see his boat.

Lonnie is an affable, solidly built man with a white beard and a ready smile.

His blue eyes twinkle as he tells us "I drink black coffee, smoke cigars and eat hot sauce on everything."

He custom designed the *Nalylo* (named after his family members) with a landing craft style ramp on the bow for easy access landing on beaches. Lonnie is a former Seabee and a licensed game transporter, dropping hunters off on remote islands. A former resident of Homer, Kodiak and Anchorage, his boat was used to shuttle the backhoe across the Kenai to work on the Russian River ferry landing.

I asked him which part of Alaska he likes the best and he instantly answers "Right here!"

We make plans to be at the boat at 6 a.m. sharp. Across the street in North Harbor, a simple handwritten cardboard sign on the road reads "Live Crabs-$5 Eldorado". We decide that crab would be a great accompaniment to our freshly caught grilled salmon.

The harbormaster directs us "All the way to the end of the pier and then turn to the right."

It's a good way down, through a forest of masts- trollers, trawlers, and the occasional mega-yacht. We pass the Silverado, Barron Hilton's luxury yacht; Lonnie says he usually spends most of the summer aboard. Kelly looks for Paris but she's not here. When we finally reach the boat the deck hand is standing next to a live well on deck that is plugged with moving Dungeness crabs.

I tell him "That's a long walk for one crab."

He smiles at my daughter and gives us 2 crabs for $5. Seems like he wants to talk, but dinner is on our minds. We walk back across the street to the fish cutting table where I filet the salmon and clean the crab. Kelly winces as I pop the top shell off, split it in two and rinse the clusters.

Annette says, "That harbor water isn't very clean, is it?"

I reply, "If it doesn't kill you, it'll make you stronger."

She doesn't smile... I rinse everything with the hose. After 25 years I've learned a valuable principle: "No happy wifee... no happy lifee..." Back at the cabin, I cook up a big batch of fried rice and we feast on our bounty- grilled silver salmon and Dungeness crab with lemon butter.

I bounce out of bed the next morning, ten minutes before the alarm goes off, because we're going fishing. When I stop doing that, it will be time to quit. At 6:02 we arrive at the harbor and Captain Lonnie is ready to go. The weather is a little less favorable than we would like, but the plan is to head out into open water to look for good sized halibut on some of the marks that he has programmed into his new GPS. The inside is calm, but as we pass between Noyes and Cone Islands, a steady stream of swells appears. These aren't the short steep troughs we have at home, but rhythmic powerful liquid hills spaced quite far apart, emanating from a storm generated in the open ocean. We prospect on 2 spots without any halibut, and Kelly is starting to look a little green around the gills. Heading toward the third hole, the swells continue to build, and Annette begins to get queasy. We decide to retreat to the inside waters. Seasickness is a horrible malady. First, you're scared that you're going to die, and then you're scared that you're going to live... and have to endure the suffering.

Lonnie is an individualist who doesn't like fishing with the pack, but he sucks it up and takes us to "The Tree" where a small flotilla of boats are catching silver salmon and a few kings. He plug-cuts herring, removing the head at a compound angle that causes the bait to spin enticingly, and briefs us on the technique of mooching for salmon.

"Drop it to the bottom, and then bring it up slowly. If you get a bite, set the hook. If it stops on the way down to the bottom, set the hook too."

Kelly once again regains her perky personality in the calmer water and is thrilled when she is the first to hook up to a feisty silver. A few minutes later, the skipper deftly spikes and swings it aboard in one smooth motion. Annette and Kelly take turns catching fish until 5 chrome beauties are chilling. Lonnie is one of the few operators who bring ice to care for the fish. Annette catches another jumbo silver. Finally, I feel a solid tug and lift the rod sharply to set the hook. It turns out to be a large pink salmon.

"Only silvers and kings get a trip to Hawaii", I tell Lonnie; he pulls the hook cleanly with his spike, and the fish swims away.

Strong swells from the open ocean begin to roll through our fishing spot, and we decide to look for halibut in the shelter of San Bautista Island. The water here is beautiful, and Kelly feels so good that she joins us in the feast that Lonnie has brought, salmon spread, halibut spread and chocolate peanut butter- all mounded up on Saloon Pilot crackers. We fill our limit with "chicken halibut"—they taste better anyway.

On the way back into the harbor, we stop at the fuel dock, and find the attendant white-faced and in a mild state of shock. He has just witnessed a float plane coming in for a landing collide with a charter boat returning from fishing.

"It took the whole cabin roof off the boat, as neat as it could be!" he exclaimed.

Fortunately, it appeared that nobody had been seriously injured, but we hear that the plane had to go back to Ketchikan to land on a foamed runway. I wonder if the passengers decided to take the ferry over after that experience.

Lonnie is disappointed that we didn't catch any large flatfish, but we are certain that he could have put us on them if the water had been more cooperative. He has a photo album of clients who made it into his "hundred pound club". The success of a fishing trip isn't measured in pounds anyway, and we do have a full box of prime salmon and halibut filets. I hope that I can fish with him again someday.

We bid farewell to the Busse family the next morning and prepare to head to Naukati. I call the Richter house to confirm that we're coming, and when Carin answers I ask if they want anything from town. She says that Greg has been having a hard time finding the "Purple" packages of large sized bait herring for Halibut. While the ladies are busy in the laundromat, I stop off to visit Lonnie and drop off a package of my spicy smoked marlin. Who brings fish *to* Alaska? He tells me that I can get a 25 pound box of jumbo sized bait herring for less than the cost of a few tray packs at the seafood processor right down the road. Such a deal.

A short time later, we're Naukati-bound, where the "disenfranchised of the world" are alleged to live. It occurs to me that a few centuries earlier the "disenfranchised of the world" also began to populate a little-known wilderness later to be known as America, and with God's help, made it a great nation.

This same anonymous source, also said that "Old man Richter, the patriarch of the community, was busted with a plane load of weed. Gives a whole new understanding of why the store is called the "Naukati Connection", doesn't it?

The October 10 issue of the POW *Island News* ran an article headlined "Local Man Sentenced in Marijuana Case". It went on to say "A Naukati man, 65 year old Allen Paul Richter has been sentenced to 46 months in prison for smuggling 405 pounds of marijuana to Nashville, Tennessee from Phoenix, Arizona... on November 27, 2004."

Our anonymous source also fills us in on the other POW scandal. The Court TV synopsis stated that "Alaska teenager Rachelle Waterman, who cast herself as a rebellious bad girl on her blog, was accused of conspiring with two ex-boyfriends to have her mother killed. The jury deadlocked, a mistrial was declared, and the charges were dropped." The verdict was pronounced on Valentine's Day of 2006.

Prince of Wales Island is not some isolated Eden insulated from the plagues of society. It is a place where people almost always wave to each other on the road and seem to have a sincere desire to help each other. There is an intangible acceptance, and apparent eagerness to engage with people who don't know you. It is refreshing. Where I live, it sometimes feels like people are enclosed in a bubble that prevents any meaningful interaction. I am reminded of an experiment in which scientists drop rats one by one into a box. At some point, they begin biting each other.

At any rate, we are leaving Klawock, bound for Naukati. The POW Chamber of Commerce web site says that "Naukati" is a native word whose meaning is unclear. Perhaps it is still in the process of defining itself. The sky drips liquid sunshine consistently as we admire the resulting rain forest. Tree covered mountains display a seemingly infinite spectrum of green and the raindrops sparkle like crystals on their branches. We cross a bridge with a sign announcing Black Bear Creek. Annette shoots me a sideways glance, and then squints her beautiful green eyes.

The pavement ends and we find ourselves on hard packed gravel. The road itself is excellent, except for the potholes. We follow the signs, and arrive at Naukati Cabins, where we check in with Art King. It is great to see him in person again with his big smile, rainbow suspenders and greeting committee of three Shih-Tzus who pirouette and frolic over and under each other, vying for our attention. It feels good to be back. The deluxe cabin, with a kitchen, shows that it has been well used in the four years since I was last here.

One of my women wrinkles her nose and wonders aloud if it "smells like bear hunters, or bear, or both."

We unload the Yukon, and then it's off to the store to look for Greg. We find his mom and his brother Andy's wife, Tamara, who tell us that he is next door in the repair shop. Greg is the best mechanic in town when he isn't the best charter boat Captain. He looks great, and I'm happy to note that I'm not the only one who has sprouted a little belly bubble. His truly boundless enthusiasm is contagious.

I tell him I've got a little present in the Yukon for him, and when he sees the 25 pound case of frozen herring, he yells out "YES!!! Now we're going to *kill* the halibut."

Kelly is a little overwhelmed by the community and the cabin and the store. "What do you do here?", she asks Brandon, Greg's 12 year old son.

"Lots of stuff", he replies "We even have mud bog races!"

"What's a mud bog?" Kelly wants to know.

It's a 3 foot deep (more or less) pit of mud 100 yards long that different classes of vehicles attempt to race through. The competition is fierce, with entries coming from all over the island.

"Want to see our bogger?" Brandon queries.

Of course we do, and it is quite a creation. It looks like a high clearance extraterrestrial vehicle for exploring a planet from a different solar system. A planet with lots of rain... and mud. The tires have rubber projections that look like fins. The bogger is obviously in the "super-modified" class. I'm a little disappointed that we will be in Point Baker the day of the next race, but we can't do everything.

"So what time are we going fishing tomorrow?", I ask Greg.

"I'll pick you up at 7:00", he responds, and then booms out "We're gonna *slay* some fish!"

It's all coming back to me, why I wanted to fish with Greg again. We return to the store to pick up a few things and see Carin. Annette invites her to come fish with us, but she has plans to drop off a vehicle at the ferry in Hollis for some guests who are coming in.

"I'll have some salmon spread for your lunch on the boat tomorrow", she says.

As we are leaving the store, Annette glimpses a young man who seems to have been smitten by my daughter. He has been staring intently at her for several minutes. Unaware that he is being watched, he literally slaps his jaw as we are leaving, and then notices that he has been seen. His cheeks are red from the slap, and from embarrassment. Poor Princess Kelly is given the title "Jaw-slapping Beauty of Naukati" for the duration of the trip.

"They don't set the bar too high here, do they?", she humbly intones.

Then we're off to the Sarkar River where Greg says we may be able to catch a silver or two on our little spinning rods. We survey the river from the bridge for several minutes.

"I'm looking for anything that's moving down there...", Annette says.

We spot three shy river otters who swirl around playfully, then dive and disappear. The three of us cautiously descend the steep slope to the river and then fling spinners into the dark tannin-stained water. On her seventh cast, Kelly nails a dime-bright silver. It jumps twice and then races upstream as the reel grudgingly gives line. It comes in prematurely, and she tries to slide it up on the rock, but it splashes back out in a flurry of foaming white water. Three minutes later she has it back. Overeager, I grab the line and pull the fish. The line goes "POP" as I pounce on the fish like a Caucasian bear who really wants fresh salmon for dinner. I'm also motivated by a desire to save the lure. Vibrax stock has probably climbed ten points since our arrival in Ketchikan. All's well that ends well, and we have beef stew, rice and fish for dinner.

The next morning I'm up early again. Greg arrives right on schedule and drives us down to the boat which is ready to go. We clamber aboard and head out the channel. Then it's a hard turn to port and we're going through Skookum Chuck and into Sea Otter Sound. We blast out through Greg's shortcut and are coming up on Black Rock in no time, where several boats are already fishing.

"A lot of lodges are making the two and a half hour run up from Craig, because they're just not catching the silvers down there this year", Greg says.

I count twelve charter boats and four power trollers working the area. It is much more crowded than the last time I was here. El Capitan even stopped broadcasting their "Today's Catch" photos over the internet, because it was attracting too many boats from distant lodges.

We begin our first drift up current from Black Rock, on the Sea Otter Sound side, and Kelly's Lamiglas rod dips sharply.

"Set the hook- *break his neck!*" Greg shouts enthusiastically.

Our first drift yields three silvers and two missed strikes. It is truly the sport of royalty to be able to pull these chrome beauties up from the depths. We continue to run up and drift down until the tide dictates that it's time to try for halibut. Ten bright salmon are in the box already. The local lodge boats swarm off the "V" on Warren Island where we used to fish, so Greg heads for a spot off of Koskiusko Island. On the first drop, I feel the tap-tap-tap of a halibut bite and focus on not pulling the hook out of his mouth. Finally, I set it and feel the solid pull of something larger than a rockfish. The head jerking thump of a halibut becomes evident. It's not a trophy, but it is a nice fish, and quickly goes into the box. We catch a few more, but Greg wants to try a different spot to see if we can find a big boy. Nobody's home, and we return to fill out our limit.

The tide change is over, so we head back to Black Rock for more silvers.

Greg solemnly intones "You have to fill up the fish box if you want to go back in... if you don't catch something soon, the Captain's going to start to twitch... and you *don't want a twitchy Captain...*"

Then he really does begin to twitch. Kelly looks a little concerned. We catch a few more salmon, and finally convince him that it's okay to go back in- we have plenty of fish.

He says, "All right, but we've got to try a little while for ling cod at a spot I know."

I miss a good bite on my first drop, but after that it's only rockfish. We make two more drifts inside Port Alice and get two more bites without hookups. It must be frustrating for Greg to watch us feed the fish. Finally, he relents, and we blast back to the dock in Naukati where his friends and family help us to cut and package the catch. Another great fishing trip!

So now we're on our way to Thorne Bay to pick up Kris, who is arriving by float plane. We elected not to tell her about the airplane and boat collision in Craig until she is with us. We stop on the road twice to photograph black tail deer, one group of three and a doe with her fawn. The drive is beautiful with vistas of tree covered mountains and many fishy looking creeks. I pull over twice to let locals go by, and we only pass a couple of dozen cars going the other way in the 44 mile road trip. We're a little early, so I seek out Jim McFarland at his Boat Works shop. He remembers me from the visit 16 years ago- that first trip. He and Jeannie are two of the "movers & shakers" in Thorne Bay with at least four businesses and a heavy involvement in community affairs. They helped to erect a welcoming kiosk at the start of town; it is an open-air shelter with a map and list of all the businesses in town. The roof of the kiosk is a gigantic mechanical log grapple which was used when the primary industry was logging.

Most of Thorne Bay appears to be freshly painted, and the majority of front yards lack the scrapyard collection of miscellaneous items evident in most other communities. I tell Jim about my observation of civic pride, and he notes that having paved roads also helps. I speak briefly with Jeannie on the phone, who is at the Floatel a couple of miles away, but she is occupied with their full booking of guests. It's the busy season, and I'm glad that they are doing so well.

The Pro-Mech float plane comes in a few minutes early, and our Kristin Leah is in the co-pilots seat with headphones on. She has earned her own private pilot's license and is in her final phase of training to become an Air Traffic Controller at Eielson AFB near Fairbanks. This was her first water landing. Everyone is ecstatic- we haven't seen her for 7 months. We bring her up to date on our adventure so far and enjoy the ride back to Naukati. I wish we had time to fish the Thorne River.

After settling in at the cabin, and touring the harbor and store, we head out to the Sarkar River to cast spinners for silvers. The fish don't cooperate, but we have a good time trying, and Kris entertains us with a fish dance intended to convince the silvers to bite. On the way back to the cabin, just before dusk, we see a bear cub on the side of the road, and a short while later, a larger black bear. The count now stands at four. After a dinner of hearty Italian sausage soup, and sautéed rockfish filets, we sleep early in anticipation of another fishing trip on the boat with Captain Greg.

A persistent mist is falling as we head out of Naukati, past Cap Island and into Sea Otter Sound. We are on plane and blasting over the glassy waters to a small rock on the backside of Warren Island in search of the elusive halibut. Greg eases off the throttle, and we bait the Gamakatsu hooks with jumbo herring, and strips of salmon belly. Greg calls the combination a "Smorgy Bob"— a smorgasbord fish-ka-bob. If the fish pulls off the soft herring it will return for the tough salmon belly still on the hook. We are drifting along with the wind and current when I feel an authoritative bump and then the rod doubles over. The ladies allow me to catch the first halibut. One more comes aboard before we reach the end of the drift and motor back to the starting point off a gravel beach. On the second drift I get another good whack and crank in a real prize.

"It's a huge yelloweye Greg; help me get it in the boat!"

The skipper handily spikes and swings it aboard. Also known as red snapper, this is the undisputed king of the rockfish family, and one of the tastiest fish in the world. The only sad note is that this fish may be fifty or more years old.

WE CONTINUE TO DRIFT as Greg skillfully backs the boat into the current to keep the lines straight down. We steadily work to fill out our limit of halibut, but when we begin to run back up to the beach, the motor makes a loud knocking sound and then dies. He restarts it, but it sputters and misses until he shuts it down.

Annette prays over it aloud "in *Jesus*' name", and the motor is born again. It roars to life and then purrs like a kitten when Greg idles it down. Nonetheless, we decide to head back closer to home, and mooch for silvers at Black Rock. There are only two other boats there, and we begin a drift on the Warren Island side. As we are closing in on the rocks, Annette and Princess Kelly get good bites. Mom's comes off, but Kelly's heads for the surface and makes three strong leaps in typical silver salmon style. Princess Leah is the next to hook up, and hers is a strong deep slugger. The rock is looming near, so Greg starts the motor and powers away slowly. After swinging another sterling silver salmon aboard, the fish box is three fourths full.

"That's your ticket home", Greg laughs "When it's topped off you can go in. I've got enough bait to stay out until midnight."

Kristin Leah retorts "If you'd take us to the right spot we'd be done already!" The poor man puts up with a lot from our middle child, and he appears to be biting his tongue a few times.

The sun peeks out of the gray sky on the edge of a "blue cloud", and Greg warns "Don't say the 's' word or it will disappear, and we won't see it the rest of the day."

Kelly asks innocently, "You mean '*sun*', is that the 's' word?"

"That's it", Greg replies drily, "I hope you got a picture with your camera, because it's gone for sure now..." Kris tells Kelly that her blonde roots are showing- that's why she said the "s" word... Our next drift is on the opposite side of the ebony island, and we score two more acrobatic silvers. Almost at the end of the drift, Kris' rod bends double as line runs out strong and steady.

"It might be a King!", Greg trumpets with enthusiasm, but the fight turns into a thumping slugfest, and our largest halibut comes to the boat on salmon gear. The day winds down as the cooler fills, and we all agree we have earned our ticket home. We are thrilled with our treasure from the sea, and the memories we've made.

AS WE PULL INTO THE dock, Greg's friends Joe, Kevin and Mike all help with the cleaning and processing, along with Carin. It's a community affair. In a flash, the fish are on their way to the freezer, and we're headed to the showers. We're going to Greg and Carin's tonight for a seafood feast, and Kevin has donated a large bag of the locally grown oysters. They are from a new aquaculture enterprise. I manage to get lost, but we finally arrive to find a huge spread of incredible edibles. Beer battered halibut, baked halibut, Kevin's homemade cheese biscuits, coleslaw and the delectable oysters.

"I put them on the grill until they pop open, and then add a few drops of teriyaki sauce", Greg says. They are plump and tasty, and I surprise myself with how many I can consume. After dinner, we watch a video segment on *Lauders Outdoors* in which Greg literally wrestles a 200 pound halibut aboard. They also caught a 180 pounder on the same trip... amazing. Kris wants to know why he didn't take us to fish there; Greg bites his tender tongue one last time. It's getting late; I call Greg's son Brandon "Drew", and call Greg "Carin"- so we know it's time to go home. It's been another long Alaska day. We thank them and wish them luck in the bog races the next day, and then bid everyone A*loha*. Later, we hear that Greg won first place in the Super Modified category.

August eleven finds us resting and getting a slow start. We drive to Coffman Cove and find it a picturesque small town clustered around the harbor. It boasts a new library and is in the process of being connected to the paved road system even having some concrete sidewalks. Everyone was in favor of eating lunch at The Cove Restaurant. Bright and cheerful, the portions were large, and the service was friendly. We stopped by the Rigging Shack, which is the grocery, dry goods, sporting goods and gift shop. Another friendly storekeeper, but the local advice was that there isn't any roadside salmon fishing close by this early in the season. We passed by the ferry terminal. Service has recently begun to Wrangell and South Mitkof Island, increasing opportunities for everyone.

After our tour of the town, it was back to the Sarkar to try to catch a salmon for dinner. We flailed the water for over an hour without a strike. Even in Alaska, fishing doesn't always mean catching—especially if you are self-guided. We usually need professional help. The consensus was to go back to the cabin, where I cooked up a big pot of halibut chowder, and sautéed Silver Salmon from yesterday's catch. Fish again, and nobody's complaining.

The next morning, we had reservations to tour the El Capitan Cave with the Forest Service guides at 9:00 a.m., so we left Naukati shortly after seven. El Cap is the largest and longest limestone grotto on POW. We meet up with a couple from Seattle who will fill up our group of five. Our two guides are pleasant and arrive right on time. They live in a trailer and tent right down the road.

THE HIKE TO THE CAVE entrance is a mini-adventure in itself. The trail is mostly uphill, including 370 stair steps on an extensive boardwalk system. Thankfully, there are frequent pauses to explain the differences between red and yellow cedar, and the variety of fern species. We finally arrive at the entrance and turn on the headlamps atop our hard hats. The first 50 yards consists of clambering over and around boulders. "Watch out for the twenty five foot deep pit on your left."

The silence is broken by Queen Annette's loud question: "Whose idea was this, anyway?"

"Mine, dear", I reply meekly, "just like coming to Alaska."

She then announces to everyone that *she* is planning the *next* vacation. The wonders of the cave prove to be worth the effort of getting there. It is amazing that underground water can create such a large cavern system. El Cap is part of what is called the "karst" system that we explore on the Beaver Falls Karst Trail- an impressive one mile boardwalk- and includes such features as sinkholes, vertical pits, and "lost rivers" like Beaver Falls, where a small river cascades down a steep hillside and then disappears into the ground below. We also hike the one tenth of a mile trail to Cavern Lake, where another small river bursts forth from a cave in the side of a mountain. Disappearing and reappearing rivers, busily creating the caves of tomorrow.

Our next stop is Whale Pass, where we tour the last community on the road system that we haven't seen. The harbor is graced with what must be the most picturesque outhouse on POW. The town is named for a ten mile strait of water between POW and Thorne Island that is frequented by Orcas and Gray Whales.

Nearby, the Neck Lake Outlet turns out to be the highlight of a very busy day. We pull over next to a bridge and a moderately busy hot dog stand, and peer down into the river to see silver salmon stacked like cord wood directly below. Upstream, Annette's eagle eye spots two small brown bears next to the hatchery. This is another very successful hatchery-enhanced fishery.

We grab our fishing poles and descend the steep path to the river. Three casts later, a very large brown bear materializes about 50 yards downstream on the opposite side. I scramble for the video camera as Queen Annette and Princess Kelly scramble back up the hill we just came down. Princess Leah pleads "Dad, can we just stay a little longer? They can wait in the car." Three of us begin to sing loudly- Kelly picks "Happy Birthday", Kris goes with "The Ants Go Marching One by One", and I choose a rousing chorus of "Jesus Loves Me". Mr. Bear closes to within 30 yards, when the cacophony literally becomes "unbearable". He ambles back the way he came.

Kris immediately catches an ambitious rainbow trout on her #5 Vibrax, which we quickly release. Then a large swirl precedes her shout of joy as a jumbo silver salmon erupts from a volcano of white froth, and slashes upstream. The silver is big and feisty, the river is small, and after three more acrobatic leaps and two more runs, it comes grudgingly to shore. In a comedy of errors, the fish is beached, squirms out of my hands, dives into the water and spits the hook. It then runs into my boot, panics and beaches itself, where I quickly two-hand-toss it up the riverbank into the rocks. I saw a bear do that once on National Geographic. It works for us as well. Kris is ecstatic- her first river silver.

• • • •

KELLY IS NOT TO BE outdone and is soon tangling with her own bundle of silver fury. It hydroplanes downstream in a flurry of white water, and then jumps straight up and shakes its head in a futile attempt to free the hook. The bank side comedy of landing the fish is reenacted with much enjoyment and approval from the spectators on the bridge.

"Maybe you should invest in a net", one remarks drily.

• • • •

WE HAVE ENOUGH FRESH salmon for dinner, so it's back up the hill for hot dogs and nachos. The juxtaposition of a hot dog stand with salmon and bears seems a bit surreal to me, but, *hey, this is Prince of Wales Island, Alaska.* Back at Naukati Cabins, we grill the fresh-as-can-be salmon with dill and lemon butter, and then pack up for our last stop on the trip... Point Baker.

We will be staying with Herb and Judy Hoyt at the Outpost Lodge. It is part of the Point Baker Trading Post, which was established in 1936. It includes a 440 foot state vessel float, which serves boats and float planes, marine fuels, showers and a laundromat, a package store and convenience store, the Baywatch Cafe, and the last "authentic" floating saloon, the Point Baker Bar, whose walls are papered with autographed dollar bills. The community consists of a large, protected bay-like area in the lee of several islands. The main attraction is a huge tidal rip at the northernmost point of the island that creates an upwelling of nutrient rich waters. This attracts the bait, and the bait attracts the predators, including salmon, rockfish, halibut and fishermen. In the 1920's and 30's, there were as many as 100 tents occupied by hand trollers who sold fish to floating fish buyers.

It is a fifteen minute boat ride from the end of the road at LaBouchere (Lab) Bay where Herb is scheduled to meet us around 11 a.m. to ferry us to the Outpost. We drive the 63 miles from Naukati to Lab Bay and see only four cars— all headed the opposite direction. In contrast, we see 15 deer on the road, all does with fawns, or yearlings. I deduce that the bucks either become educated early or become venison. We bump over the last pothole and find Herb holding the bowline of Judy's 21foot Glasply. We are soon aboard and leaving the road system behind. This is the Real Alaska. Judy is there to greet us, and we all seem like old friends in a matter of minutes. Herb and Judy's incredible resourcefulness is evident as soon as you arrive. In addition to managing the myriad enterprises, they run their own power and water plants. No wonder Herb says that he doesn't have time to fish.

After we have settled in, I check out the galley, where I have volunteered to be a guest chef for a night and prepare dinner with a Hawaiian flair. Kelly and Kris are drafted, and we serve appetizers of smoked marlin, followed by entrees of Teriyaki Venison, Furikake Rice Seasoning Baked King Salmon, and Panko Crusted Halibut with wasabi spiced Red Menace Sauce. We are scheduled for a full day charter with Captain Lee Carroll on his Grady-White boat, the *Hot Rod*, tomorrow. He joins us for dinner, and the company and conversation are fascinating. The evening ends much too soon.

The next morning, Herb is up early, preparing biscuits and gravy, eggs, and even a fresh pineapple that we didn't bring from home. The world really is shrinking quickly. Soon, we're idling out of the harbor and when we reach the open water, Captain Lee opens up the throttles on the twin 200 horse outboards. We are blasting south on plane to a spot he calls the "Holly Hole", where his daughter caught a 120 pound halibut. Lee is a meticulous and proficient skipper, and soon the women are hooking up all around me, with good sized halibut for the freezer. My technique of raising and lowering the bait is not working at all, and the ladies are quick to point it out. They have five nice flat fish tied to the side of the boat when something different grabs Kris' bait and attention. The head thumping of the halibut is replaced with strong hard runs that bend the rod impressively. A nice ling cod comes grudgingly to the boat, and fortunately fits into the 30 to 40 inch slot size limit.

"Do you folks eat these?" Captain Lee asks enthusiastically. "They make great fish and chips!" We nod in agreement. The women begin to tease me mercilessly about my inability to catch any fish. Kris says it's because she has my lucky orange beanie on, and Kelly quickly snatches it off her head and puts it on, as Annette hooks another halibut. A curious sea otter swims nearby and entertains us with an aquatic ballet. We ask Captain Lee if that's a regular part of the program, and he replies that you never know what might happen. He tosses the otter a herring in appreciation of the performance.

The tide has changed, and the current begins to run like a river, so we opt to troll for salmon. As soon as Lee gets the downriggers set, Annette's pole goes off, and a silver bullet gives a spectacular show of six strong jumps. One of the fattest silvers of the trip is her prize. We troll our way back up to the lodge, hooking and releasing a couple of pinks. We keep a bright chum salmon that impresses us with its strong and powerful runs. When we get back to the point, we troll around the rip and catch more pink salmon, and rockfish, but the silver salmon and kings are missing in action.

As we approach the choppy waves that designate where the two currents form the rip, a whale broaches close to the boat, and from that time on, the trip becomes a whale watching tour for Princesses Kelly and Leah. Kris calls the whales, imitating Dora from *Finding Nemo,* and waves her arms like a flying bird pretending to be the *Whale Rider.* She names one whale "Quasi", and another "Moto", and calls for them repeatedly. Kelly bursts into laughter and informs her that "Quasimoto" is the *hunchback* of Notre Dame, not the *humpback.*

"Same smell," Kris retorts sassily. Cameras in hand, they continue to enjoy literally dozens of sightings.

When a mother and calf appear only 25 feet from the boat, Kelly pronounces "This is *so* magical." We all agree. The sun is out, the sky is blue, and our adventure is complete. We cruise slowly back to the float with a deep sense of satisfaction and reverence for what a special place this is.

Judy is at the dock to greet us as Lee unloads our catch. "Looks like you had a fun day," she comments.

Lee responds, "It's a show watching these folks."

THEY WERE RIGHT ON both counts. Captain Lee and I quickly clean all the fish and get them in the freezer, so that he can get back to his wife and home in Wrangell. Before he leaves, he generously asks Herb and Judy to give us a couple large packages of King Salmon filets that they are storing for him.

OUR "LAST SUPPER" IS a glorious feast of Dungeness Crab Appetizers, followed by Shrimp Alfredo with Pasta. It's hard to believe that shellfish can be so sweet. The stay at Point Baker flies by too quickly, and the evening does as well. The next morning, we are up early for a marathon day- we have to catch the 2:30 ferry at the other end of the island in Hollis. After another of Herb's lumberjack breakfasts, we bid aloha to Judy and depart. The tide is high, so Herb gives us a tour through the back end of the inlet, and I even get to see Joe Upton's old cabin. It was his book <u>Alaska Blues</u> that brought me and my family here. Another case of the experience being worth the trip. Then it's back to Lab Bay, where even more adventure awaits.We say goodbye to Herb, and I climb up the hill to bring our trusty Yukon down to load up. I turn the key... and nothing happens. I holler down the hill, and then all four of us are yelling for Herb to come back. Our chorus is joined by a couple who live in a floating cabin in the bay, and fortunately Herb hears them. The good neighbors have a jumper cable, and Herb has a battery. Thankfully, the engine starts. You wanted adventure- you get adventure. We thank everyone and say goodbye again. As we start down the road, the Yukon begins to cough whenever I let up on the accelerator. Finally, it sputters and dies at the bottom of a hill. My expletives have been deleted from this account but trust me that they were colorful. My heart sinks deep into the pit of my stomach.

"Have faith", Annette says, and then asks me to pray.

After repenting for my outburst and petitioning the Lord yet again for a recalcitrant motor, the engine roars to life, and performs flawlessly the rest of the day. We stop at Naukati to pick up the rest of our fish from Art's chest freezer and load them into our styrofoam lined fish boxes. Then it's a few more bumpy miles back to the paved road. Our next stop is the laundromat in Craig where we use their scale to repack our fish boxes to the maximum weight of 69 pounds. I overhear a guide from a local lodge lamenting the shortage of silver salmon this year.

"The only place with a steady run seems to be Black Rock, and that's a long way to go."

Yes Mr. Guide— it is a long way from Craig, but it's very close to Naukati... Sounds like a good reason to *go* there. It's even *closer* to Edna Bay or Cape Hole. Perhaps they will become the *new* Naukati. Then, maybe I can flock there with the other disenfranchised of the world. Sounds like a plan.

We have a few extra packages of salmon, so we drop them off at the Trophy Lodge for the Busse family. They were so hospitable to us. We are now running *really* late, even by McCrone standards, and it's a race to the ferry. We make it with two minutes to spare and are thankful that we already have our tickets. Fish and baggage aboard, it is a relaxing three hours to Ketchikan. Then we are back at The Landing, Halibut Olympia at Jeremiah's, and a restful night's sleep.

The next morning, we are on the first shuttle bus trip to the airport ferry and give the driver a box of chocolate covered macadamia nuts.

"That's Chicken", he intones solemnly, and we think that must be a good thing.

We see our friend from the ferry on the outbound trip, Sal Williams, dropping off a fare in his taxi, and give him a box, too. I hope he gets to move back to the Island. Thank goodness that they finally got baggage carts at the ferry landing. We stevedore our luggage and, yes, *seven* fish boxes to the check in. Seven is the number of perfection remember? Then we're waiting in the terminal for takeoff. We say goodbye to Kris who is northbound to Fairbanks. She is rated as an Air Traffic Controller in less than a month.

All good things come to an end, and this vacation is one of them. I got to return to Prince of Wales and see the whole island, from Hydaburg to Lab Bay, and points beyond. I not only caught a giant yelloweye rockfish, but also learned valuable lessons about stalking the elusive artist's conch. (Keep your mouth closed when prying it off the tree!) I'm still looking for a cabin... Annette overcame all her fears and had a surprisingly good time. She especially enjoyed the tranquility of fishing for silver salmon in the rivers. Although we did see at least nine bears, and lots of "sign" (if you know what I mean), we didn't have any close encounters of the worst kind. Kris fit back into the family as if she had never been gone and kept us entertained with her fish dance and whale watching antics. Quasimoto?- The humpback of Notre Dame? Who *are* the parents? Princess Kelly also enjoyed herself immensely. She caught her first salmon and halibut and also earned her new title as "The Jaw-Slapping Beauty of Naukati".

A lot of things happened on this trip to the Great Land— incredible scenery, lots of wildlife, a unique cast of characters, and great fishing. But the best part was being there... *together.*

• • • •

Magic Bull Moment

First published in The Alaska Sporting Journal October 2014

"DID YOU HEAR THAT?" It is 3:50 AM on a frosty early September in the Alaskan interior. My hunting partner, Lenny DiPaolo and I switch on flashlights and reach for our .44 magnum handguns simultaneously. A branch breaking close to the tent has roused us from a fitful slumber.

"What do you think that was?" I know what we both are thinking.

It is day four of our hunt. We've driven from our homes in Kasilof on the Kenai Peninsula, to Delta Junction, and flown out with Golden Eagle Outfitters for a fly-in float-out hunt. Pilot Jim Cummings takes us to the headwaters of a tributary of the Tanana River. We need four trips in one of his Super Cubs to get us and our gear to a spot above the reach of the jet boats that ply the river during moose season.

We plan to float, and motor when possible, all the 105 river miles to where my truck awaits at the bridge near Delta Junction.

On day one, Lenny is the first to be dropped off on the tiny landing strip. As soon as the Super Cub takes off a brown bear ambles across the clearing. As he reaches for his rifle it melts into the trees. *Let the adventure begin!*

A slow and steady drizzle is falling as I am flown in on the last trip. Jim lifts the tail and spins the Super Cub around, and then takes off. We are alone. Check that... very alone. We awaken to the steady drip of a serious rain. Somehow, the tarp we placed over the tent allows water to seep in and soak the floor and our sleeping bags. We inflate the Pioneer Pro raft and load up for our first day of floating. At least the coffee is hot.

"If it's moose season it has to be raining", Lenny concludes. "That's the rule."

He rows while I sit in the front with my father's heirloom, a Winchester Model 70 .30-06. Lenny had been a fishing guide on the Kasilof River for a number of years, and his expertise on the oars is invaluable on this trip. A few miles downstream we spot a trapper's cabin and pull in. The opportunity to regroup and dry our gear by a fire is irresistible. I find a shed caribou antler where we pull out, and we scout the game trails next to the river. Caribou bulls are legal here with a registration permit, but we only see a few moose tracks, bear tracks and scat. Early the next morning we climb to a clearing overlooking 100 acres of prime habitat, but nothing

is moving. Back at camp, we catch two fat grayling in a few casts and feast on fresh fish with ramen noodles.

DAY THREE FINDS US packing up in the dark, hoping for a magical moment while floating in the early morning. The river is skinny in places, and we must get out and pull the raft by hand. As we come to a fork, Lenny chooses to go to the right, we drop down a chute with a 90 degree turn to the left and run directly into a deadfall that is blocking the way. There is nothing we can do but cut the tree out of the way with a Wyoming saw, a heavy duty tool used to cut bones and firewood, among other tasks. There are also sweepers, snags and logjams ahead of us. We stop to scout likely spots and find some evidence of moose, but there is more bear sign than anything else. Late in the afternoon, we come to an area where three recently burned hillsides converge. We decide to camp there and climb to the ridge in the morning. At least that was the plan before our mysterious 4:00 a.m. wakeup call. Discretion being the better part of valor, we decide to pack up and float down to what we hope is a more moose friendly environment. First light finds us on the river. Meandering through a long low and swampy valley, an inviting gravel bar choked with willow and alder beckons. As I scout upstream and down, Lenny rakes the bushes with the shed caribou antler, imitating a bull scraping the velvet off his rack. I find more moose tracks, but none of them have hooves in them. We clamber back into the raft, and drift about fifty yards. Rounding a bend, Lenny stage whispers the words I have been waiting for.

"*Right there! Big bull moose!*"

He must have heard Lenny thrashing the bushes and come out to see what the ruckus was about. This bull is a magnificent animal, standing at the edge of the river, about 150 yards away. I turn the dial on my scope from 3X to 6X and rest the rifle barrel on the dry bag in the bow of the raft. It is every bit as good as a bench rest. The raft is pointing toward the bank, and my body is twisted, so I look back at Lenny. His hands are cupped over his ears.

"Point me toward him, Lenny," I whisper.

With a deft stroke of the oar, he does just that. We bounce over a shallow riffle, causing my crosshairs to bounce from his shin to over his shoulder. "*I have to wait*", I tell myself. He spots us and turns to walk into the forest just as the water flattens. Finally able to hold steady behind his shoulder, and gently squeezing the trigger, the rifle cracks with authority. The bull hunches, then spins around and lunges into the water, coming to rest about ten feet from the bank. I am trembling. It is a bittersweet moment with conflicting emotions, from a feeling of success, elation, and relief, to one tinged with sorrow to see the demise of such a magnificent creature. This animal is a gift. I place my hand on his broad shoulder and give thanks. This moose will feed our families through the cold dark winter and beyond.

FORTUNATELY, WE HAVE a continuous feed winch and pull our trophy up on the bank in about an hour. It takes another five hours to skin, quarter and remove the meat from the carcass, and finally load it onto the raft. Floating until almost dark, we pull out on a gravel bar and construct a sturdy meat pole supported by two log tripods. The bags are well-chilled in the forty degree air. Lenny and I gather an enormous pile of logs and keep a bonfire going all night. We are not necessarily the apex predators on this gravel bar, so nobody sleeps. On the river at first light, we row and motor for fifteen and a half hours to our takeout at the bridge in Delta Junction. We arrive as two tired, thankful and happy hunters.

2014

We are launching from the beach and our daughter Kris makes a facebook post with this picture and the following, "If I am never seen again, I was last seen with this man, halibut fishing in the open ocean in a rowboat."

ANNETTE AND I HAVE had the commercial charter boat experience several times. Some were good trips, a couple were great, and some, not so much. The less than stellar ones consist of waking up way too early and driving the sixty miles to Homer, then pounding away on the open ocean for an hour or more, only to arrive at a place where a dozen other boats are fishing. The water is 200 feet deep, the weights are three to five pounds, and the fish are not very big. After pulling the heavy weights up for a couple of hours, the tide has turned, and the current is becoming too strong to keep even the ponderous weights on the bottom.

"Ten minutes, and we have to head back", says the deckhand. "Keep what you catch or go back with nothing." And did I mention the cost?

We met Rick and Barb Larson at Soldotna Bible Chapel. He was one of the ushers, and a mutual acquaintance who I bought my drift boat from, told me that he is an avid and very successful fisherman. Rick said that, on a good weather day, they launch their drift boats from a beach on Cook Inlet and catch halibut within a mile of shore. I am all ears. It takes some smooth talking and persistence to assuage the blushing bride's apprehensions, but eventually she agrees to "try it once". That is all it takes for us to realize what a unique and wonderful opportunity is available to us. On our premiere voyage we catch a seventy four pound fish, and are hooked for life.

A few weeks later, our daughter Kris agrees to join us. Sam will have the kids for the day. We meet the Larsons on the beach at 7:00 am, just at the peak of high tide. We work together to slide our boats the few feet down to the ankle high waves. The water is glassy, and Mount Augustine and Mount Iliamna are perfectly reflected. We have a tide change of only eight feet today, which means that the current will not be very strong, allowing us to hold bottom with lighter weights and to go back into shore at any time. On a day when the tide goes from -4 feet to +20 feet, it is difficult to keep your bait on the bottom, even with twenty ounces of lead, and it is also challenging to row against the flow. The boat travels one foot up or down the beach for every foot gained coming in. Also, at any tide smaller than +2 feet, a sandbar is exposed which prevents us from getting to shore. We will have to wait for at least one hour before or after a negative tide to clear the bar. In short, the conditions are perfect today. I point the bow of the boat towards Augustine, and then find a landmark on shore that is in the center of the stern to maintain a straight course while rowing backwards. I maintain a steady pace until we are at an imaginary line that runs from Ninilchik to Anchor Point.

"Drop the anchor", I say, and the first mate and bosun leap to it.

We have a Danforth anchor with eight feet of chain, and a mesh bag is attached just above the chain, which is filled with chopped up red salmon carcasses. The water depth is about fifty feet.

I grab Annette's rod first and take her leader out of the sandwich bag. It has a large circle hook on a four foot leader of 200 pound test line with a four inch lead line attached to a triangle three way swivel that we get in Hawaii. These special swivels prevent the line from wrapping and tangling going up and down. The hook is baited with half of a large herring. The point goes through twice, once above the spine and the other below. We will use a six ounce cannonball sinker at this stage of the tide so that the bait scopes out with the current to get an optimal distance of fifty feet, or so, behind the boat. Too heavy of a lead keeps the bait close where boat shy fish might not venture. Too light of a weight, and the bait will travel too far too fast, or might not even hit bottom. As the strength of the pull increases with the tide change, the weight size is increased to achieve a steady contact with the bottom while still scoping out for the hunting halibut to intercept. Kris is set up next, and then it's my turn. My leader has the addition of a "palu bag". This is a cone shaped piece of duck cloth, about ten inches long, with a six inch tapered flap extending on the open end. The pointed end of the cone is attached to a three way swivel on the main line, about six feet above the leader with the hook. Palu is the Hawaiian verb for "to smash", and the noun definition is "chum". I have a two gallon bucket containing five pounds of herring that has been coarsely ground, and then mixed with five pounds of sand. I use a pointing trowel to fill the bag with chum and tuck in the flap to enclose it. When the lead hits the bottom, I reel up three turns and then jerk the rod sharply a few times to pop the flap open and disperse the chum. Halibut fishermen have many creative and diverse ways of chumming, but the common denominator is that the most successful ones employ some method like this to attract fish. One must be careful that the chumming is not excessive, or the fish will simply wait for chum and bite tentatively, or not at all. There is a fine line between chumming effectively and feeding the fish.

The Larsons are anchored about three hundred yards away from us, further out and closer to Ninilchik. They have an outboard motor that I am trying hard not to covet. I hear a distinct and rapid drumbeat coming from their direction which means they already have a keeper in the cooler. It's probably Barb who caught it, although Rick is a great fisherman in his own right. I am dropping down a fresh bait. It hits the bottom, and I reel up three turns and then pop the palu bag. Keeping the reel in free spool, with my thumb on the line, I lift and then release the line to allow the current to drift the bait away from the boat. The bait is traveling in the direction that the chum was dispersed. After the seventh lift and release, the rod tip jiggles, and there is something alive on the other end. This is when it gets tricky. Lift too quickly, and you pull the bait out of the fish's mouth. Wait too long, and the halibut steals the bait, gets full and swims away. The conventional wisdom, fishing with circle hooks, is to let the fish hook itself. Multiple deck hands on commercial charter boats have told me the same thing. "Don't jerk! Let the fish eat the bait. If you think it has it, wait for a pull, then lift the rod and reel the line. If it goes slack, drop it back down and wait. There's a good chance the fish will come back."

I follow the conventional wisdom, and have my bait stolen. Again... Fortunately, Annette has a rod thumper. It did not play the nibbling game- it hit the bait hard and swam away, firmly setting the hook in the corner of its jaw. It is pulling line against the drag, and obviously a keeper. In a few minutes, she has it up to the side of the boat. I open the cooler, grab the leader and use the stainless steel meat hook to welcome it aboard. Fish for dinner! The Hawaiian tradition is to kiss and release the first fish so that it will tell the others to bite. We are *not* Hawaiians. This halibut weighs respectable twenty pounds and we are off to a great start. Kris and Annette each catch small ones, which we release boat side. Both of them are in the eight to ten pound range, and either would have been considered "keepers" in Hawaii, but we're not in Kansas anymore, Toto.

"First you catch the small ones, and then the big ones come", I intone. Sometimes that's true. Kris is getting a bite also, now. Her rod tip twitches and then stops. An excruciating ten seconds later, it twitches again, and then her rod bends. She lifts and reels, and, as conventional wisdom would have it, she has a fish on. This one is also a keeper and joins the other in the cooler.

"Only four more, and we can go in", I say.

"Feel free to make a contribution there, Pooter-Pop!" my sassy daughter taunts.

Redemption comes shortly thereafter. I make a drop and start scoping out the line. After the fourth lift of the rod and release, there is no tension on the line. A fish has taken the bait and is swimming toward the boat.

"Hanapa'a!" I yell out "Fish On!"

This is the largest so far. I reel it up halfway, and then hand the rod to Kris, who occupies the seat on the same side that I am facing.

"Bring it up slowly; I gotta get ready."

This one is a harpooner— over thirty pounds. The harpoon point is affixed to twelve inches of braided wire with a loop on each end and tied to 100 feet of nylon cord. The cord is stowed in a large plastic coffee can with the tag end tied to the footrest on the bottom of the boat. I see the bag coming up and then the fish.

"Nice halibut... go slow."

Placing the harpoon tip on the shaft and holding it in place with tension from the cord on the harpoon handle, I reach for the leader as the fish continues to come up easily. At the surface, I slack the pressure to keep its head in the water. It levels out, and the harpoon is thrust through the gill plate, just forward if the pectoral fin. The point pivots sideways, so that it cannot come out. On the surface, the halibut gives Kris and I a shower with its tail splashing and then pulls line from the reel and the cord through my gloved left hand. Afterwards, Kris reels as I pull the cord. At the side of the boat, the meat hook and rope are used to slide the fish in with the others. I close the lid quickly as the fish pummels the cooler top on its way to halibut Valhalla. A large bungee cord is attached over the top of the cooler, from handle to handle, until the pounding ends. Afterwards I untie the harpoon head and slide the loop end through the fish, then unhook and bleed it by cutting the gills. And now, Kris has a puzzled look on her face. "Are we drifting? My line went slack."

Mine has also gone slack. On a large tide change the Danforth anchor can slip, but it is unusual on a day with this amount of tide change. "Reel in the slack; maybe the anchor will grab again."

I retrieve the excess line and regain tension with the weight, but Kris is still reeling. Suddenly, her rod is bent over double and line is smoking off the reel. Whatever is on the other end is large and in charge. Then, the line goes slack again. "Did it come off?" My question is answered when the rod is once again bent double.

"This is really weird, dad."

Finally, our quarry is close, and we are eager to see it. "Color!", I exclaim as it appears, my harpoon in hand.

That's when it got scary. A six foot Salmon Shark, as big around as a 54 gallon drum, appears out of the depths, swimming straight towards the boat. It hunches its back and lunges forward— just like the ones attacking on Shark Week, and then literally spits the hook out right at the boat. We are all dumfounded and speechless. Finally, I break the silence. *"We need a bigger boat..."*

Annette asks Kris to pull the anchor so that we can redeploy it. "Holy shiitake mushrooms; I'm not touching anything near the water!" is her response.

The anchor mystery is solved when we pull it up. The shark had savaged the chum bag so aggressively that the anchor lost its hold. We have now replaced the Danforth with a Kenai River Style Anchor which is heavier, but never slips.

Looking at the Larsons boat, everyone is standing up and Rick has the harpoon out. Then, suddenly, water is exploding everywhere. Shortly thereafter we see him slide a dandy halibut over the side. We have only been on the water a few hours and the action is nearly non-stop. We catch and release two more, and then keep one that is about fifteen pounds. Another one about the same size comes up. "That's bigger than my frying pan", I say as it goes in the cooler.

I call Rick and he affirms that they also only need one more fish as Annette's rod is pulled down hard with line stripping off the reel in steady pulses. This is surely the biggest fish of the day. After about ten minutes, we can see the mottled green form coming up. I harpoon it, and it doesn't even attempt to swim away. It is a gift. There is just enough room in the cooler to be able to close the top, and when I do, the halibut comes out of its catatonic state and attempts to shatter the cooler into pieces, The lid flies open, and I slam it shut and attach the bungee cord. We are tired and happy!

Our able deckhands pull the anchor, and as I row for shore, we see the Larsons piping aboard their fourth and final fish. Everyone is ecstatic on the beach with the magnitude of our blessings and the beauty of our surroundings. We take the obligatory photos to prove that this was not just a great dream, and then set up the tables to filet the fish and get them ready for vacuum sealing and freezing at home. What a Great Day!

When our son-in-law Sam hears about our day, his response is classic. "Wow, that's really cool. Halibut on the cheap. I think I'll look for a drift boat." I reply, "I think we'll look for an outboard motor."

Reunion of the F/ V
Hoku O Ke Kai

2014 Forty years or so ago, Co-Captains Augie and Moses trained a greenhorn deckhand in the pursuit of giant 'ahi and marlin in the land that once was paradise. It was the late seventies, when Les Walls, the radio announcer who gave fishing reports proclaimed:

"It's the fourth of July. If you fished out of Pokai Bay today and ran a pink and white jet head and *didn't* catch a hundred pound 'ahi, you should quit fishing!"

These were the days of abundance before the fleets of longliners reduced the tuna population from a flood to a trickle.

I'm in my mid-twenties when my parents buy a house in Mililani Town, for the exorbitant price of $76,000. I have failed to launch and am still living at home, working as an apprentice tile setter and saving for a down payment to buy a house of my own. Our neighbor across the street is Augustine Anthony Gouveia III— "Augie", and he and his fishing partner Moses Nishii have just bought a boat! It is a rather unusual fishing boat, a Wellcraft Nova 250 Offshore, with a large inboard motor and a hull style resembling a Cigarette Racing Boat. The Hawaiian name translates as *Star Of The Sea,* a rather ostentatious moniker. Augie and Moses are both flight attendants for United Airlines and have schedules that give them several days off in which they can fish. I tell Augie how much I love fishing and he invites me to go with him and Moses out of Waianae.

We clear the harbor and Captain Augie says: "Breaker, breaker 23, this is KBFZ2760, the Hoku O Ke Kai, looking for a radio check, anybody got a copy?"

"Roger, Hoku O Ke Kai, you're coming in loud and clear."

"Mahalo for the check, channel clear."

Outside the harbor, we head south and troll the waters between Nanakuli and the Power Plant- Marlin Country. The lure on the short outrigger gets hammered and an angry Pacific Blue Marlin is tail dancing behind the boat!

Moses and I clear the other rods and stow them, and then they let me fight the fish. It seems huge. After a half hour, the beast is coming close and tiring. Moses leaders the fish and Augie leaves the steering wheel long enough to sink the first gaff, then Moses gets the second in. It is my first marlin over a hundred pounds.

Three is the optimal number for crew on a trailer boat- one to drive, one to be the leader man and another to gaff. I am ecstatic to be accepted as a junior member of the crew. On another solo trip, Augie and I catch an 'ahi fishing out of Kaneohe that tipped the scales at Nanko Fishing Supply at 232 pounds, one of the most epic and challenging catches of my life. This fish was caught on the first Magic Lure of four that I have encountered. The slang Hawaiian expression for a sure thing is "Garanz Ball Bearins", and this lure was nicknamed the "Garanz" after the first time it was run. Augie and Moses were fishing an 'ahi school with another boat when their long outrigger lines became entangled. Somehow, when Moses reeled in, there was a lure from the other boat tangled on the line. It had a clear fiberglass head with some sort of fabric that turned color from red to blue to green, yellow and purple. It had four small tubes to create a bubble trail with wings made of the same color-changing fabric. It was skirted with blue and silver. The lure looked alive in the water and caught many 'ahi and other fish until it was lost to an ono strike.

Bottom fishing at Kaena Point, we caught a 74 pound ulua, and on another trip had a fourteen foot Tiger Shark eat a papio (jack) literally eight feet from the boat. I quit night diving after that experience. We had several great years of fishing together, but then I got married and moved out, and Augie moved to Washington state. I learned a great deal from these guys.

I had the privilege of fishing in the Kona Gold tournament with them and Ed Jensen, nicknamed "Champ". We had a great stay at his house and several great days of fishing, although we didn't catch any qualifying fish during the tournament. One day we followed a school of jumbo sized aku- "otaru"- and had some of the best poke' and sashimi of my life. Good times! Champ caught the marlin in the photo from Kona.

Great memories!

AUGIE AND I MADE A ten day trip to the Kenai with Clayton Tanaka and Kevin Dimond, and had a great time fishing for sockeye, even doing an overnight halibut trip out of Homer. Augie and Moses had a few Alaska trips together on the Situk River in Yakutat, fishing for reds.

FAST FORWARD FORTY years and I invite Augie and Moses to come for a week and fish with me in the Great Land. On the first day we float down the upper Kasilof, stopping at Bear Corner for a few reds. I keep looking over my shoulder there for some reason. We get a few more at the gravel bar across from our house, but it isn't a day to catch our limits. It is, however, more than enough for a tasty dinner.

The next day is calling for great weather conditions on Cook Inlet, so the plan is to launch from the beach in a quest for flatfish. We are up early for the forty mile drive south to my favorite spot. We are launching near the peak of high tide, so we don't have to push the boat very far to reach the water. Augie is the first to put one in the boat, followed pretty close by Moses. Finally, something is jiggling my rod tip and I am able to hook it. It's not a giant, but it is a keeper. The waves are starting to pick up,

and there are a few whitecaps, so we keep the next three fish and head back to shore. It's an awfully big ocean in an eighteen foot drift boat. We land on the beach and clean the fish, then it's back to beautiful downtown Kasilof. Later, while we are vacuum sealing the fish, there seems to be some tension about who will get to keep the halibut cheeks.

"How long have you guys been married?", I ask drily.

"Too long", is the answer. And then we all laugh. It's great to be with the guys again.

We are back on the river the next day and the run has picked up. The limit for sockeye has also been raised from three to six fish. Augie and Moses both are hooking fish consistently and it is a lot more fun than the first day. We end the day with enough to smoke a batch, so I brine the filets and put them in the refrigerator to marinate overnight. We have another successful red trip the next day and it looks like the guys will have a respectable amount of fish to take back. We have a beautiful blue-sky short-sleeve shirt weather day to fish for sockeye. The boat is tied up right below the house, so we walk down the 61 steps, clamber in and I row across the river to the gravel bar. The fishing is a little tougher today, but we manage a respectable catch after flipping for seven hours. We really had to work for them today.

THE WEATHER IS LOOKING good again for halibut. We clean the boat and switch gear for saltwater fishing. During these long days of summer fish camp, we go and go until we have nothing left and sometimes it impacts my cognitive ability. I have forgotten to bring essential pieces of the halibut gear on a few occasions. Once it was the gas tank, so I had to row like I did in our early days, before we got the outboard motor. Another time I left the anchor at home and we had to tie a bucket to the stern to slow the drift. The next time it was the harpoon, but fortunately (or unfortunately) we didn't get any big ones that day, anyway. One other time, I was pushing the boat down to the water with my friend Rick and asked him how he liked my new rubber boots. I was wearing sneakers—my boots were still at home. I have a checklist now that I go over before we leave, and it really has been helpful. We have a sign in our kitchen that states: "Fish, Eat, Sleep, Repeat". Maybe we should add in "Rest".

At the beach it's another gorgeous day weather wise, and the water is calmer as well. We motor out for ten minutes and drop the anchor. I do three quick drops with the chum bag to get some scent in the water, and shortly afterwards we are rewarded with nibbles on both Augie and Moses' rods. Augie hooks his fish, but Moses gets robbed.

"Let me know if you need some coaching, Moses", Augie taunts. I can't seem to buy a bite, so I bite my tongue. Moses redeems himself shortly afterwards with a nice fish and asks Augie if he wants to know how to catch the bigger fish. We let two little guys go and then I catch a keeper. There is a lull in the action, and we reminisce about the good old days and lament how the fishery in Hawaii has declined. We remember with fondness how every boat could catch a hundred pound yellowfin in July. Augie and Moses would always keep the first 'ahi of the season to cut up and share with family and neighbors. We all agree that the secret to catching a lot of fish is to be generous in giving it away. Our conversation is terminated by a serious bend in Augie's rod with line hissing off the reel. It is a thumper! After about ten minutes a very respectable sized halibut comes to the boat and I'm able to harpoon it and slide it over the side and into the cooler. Shortly afterwards Moses and I both get our last fish, and we are done for the day. They are all good eating size. We are tired and happy. These are still the good old days.

2015

"Ellen and Kevin are coming! They made their reservations!"

My blushing bride is ecstatic. One of her hanabada friends (Hawaiian for they've known each other since snot-nosed small-kine kid days) is coming to visit us. Annette has three BFF's with whom she can talk on the phone for an hour or more, but this one in particular, is very adventurous. When they were teenagers, they flew to Molokai unescorted, with one-way tickets, and had to bag kiawe (mesquite) charcoal in order to earn money for the flight home. They stayed with a Baha'i couple who lived off the grid. Annette blew out a flip-flop and hobbled around for a while. I'm not sure that Kevin and Ellen's adventure in the Great Land will rival this one, but we look forward to seeing them. Kevin is a brawny, easygoing and very affable guy and we get along great.

"When is the best time to come?", they asked.

"The peak of the fishing season is the last two weeks of July. The Red-Sockeye Salmon- season can continue to peak for two more weeks, but fishing for King Salmon ends on the 31st of July. We will be harvesting the first of our veggies and berries from the garden and greenhouse then, too."

Kevin and Ellen live in Rohnert Park, California, near the heart of Wine Country, and they arrive with a styrofoam wine case holding a dozen bottles. We are going to be stepping up our exposure to fine wines, and I have a few humble homemade varieties made with our own berries to add to the collection. It's going to be a good time! And we will be fishing! No fishing and drinking, though. The first adventure is in pursuit of king salmon on the world-famous Kenai River. Our good friends, Rick and Barb Larson have offered to take Kevin on their boat on "Drift Boat Monday", the 27th of July. The river is closed to fishing from power boats on every Monday in June and July, so that we can have the exclusive use of the river without constantly being bounced around by power boats. My drift boat is only 18 feet, stem to stern, and can only accommodate two anglers comfortably (three if one is very small) and the oarsman. A boat has been accurately defined as "a hole in the water that you throw money into." Our boat creates a very small hole, and we are okay with that.

We will be launching our drift boats at 6:00 a.m. at a "secret spot" launch site, and taking out at Eagle Rock, about six river miles away. After temporarily interrupting the sockeye fishermen who were flipping from shore, we are headed downstream. One of the best king salmon holes on the river is less than a half mile away— Big Eddy. The main current breaks at the end of this hole with most of the water continuing downstream, but some of it turns into a slough in a counter current. The fishing drill consists of rowing against the main current at the top of the hole to slow the drift of the boat while the anglers drop cured salmon eggs behind a spin-n-glo attractor. The correct amount of weight will allow the offering to stay on the bottom while scoping out about twenty feet in front of the boat. At the end of the hole, I row into the counter current and back up the slough to start the circuit again. I have never caught a fish, or rowed while anyone caught a fish, in this hole before, but there's a first time for everything. I anchor the boat out of the main current to rig the rods and brief Annette and Ellen.

"The idea is to let out enough line to get the eggs out in front of the boat and then tap the bottom steadily. If you feel any resistance, jerk hard to set the hook."

We make the first circumnavigation of Big Eddy behind Rick, and neither of us has any action. The girls' baits seem to be staying too close to the boat, so I switch the weights from five ounces to four before the next go-round. On this pass, we are halfway down the drift, on the seam where the swift water kisses the calm water, and opposite a whitewashed log on the gravel bar, when Ellen's rod bends sharply.

"Set the hook and reel!" I yell excitedly.

She does, and we have a solid hookup. Annette takes the landing net and holds it up in the air so that the other boats will know that we have a fish on and stay clear. We see envious looks from all six of the other drift boats in the hole. It appears that the tension on the drag is set correctly, allowing the fish to take line grudgingly, but neither too tight nor loose. I row for the slack water in the slough, where we will not have to fight the current to net the fish.

"Lift the rod, and then reel down, keeping the rod bent", I tell Ellen, and she does an excellent job— steady and smooth.

We have color and see that it is a very large chrome bright trophy, fresh from the sea, when it makes a final strong run, peeling line from the reel. Ellen retrieves the line up to the swivel.

"Bring your rod tip over my head, and when the fish is over the net, drop it and give me slack." She does and we have our prize in the net. High fives all around!

"I have good news and bad news for you, Ellen. The good news is that you caught a king; the bad news is that you're done fishing for the day..."

We rebait Annette's rig and get ready to slide back into the procession of boats. The Larson's boat gives us thumbs up as we pass by, and you couldn't wipe the smile off my face with a scrub brush. On the very next pass, in nearly the same exact spot, the Blushing Bride's rod kisses the water and line is escaping at an alarming rate as the fish heads downstream in the fast current.

"Reel fast and keep the line tight, I'm going to get ahead of it."

Ellen raises the net as I head off the fish and maneuver to pull it into the back current. If it escapes the calm water in the hole, it will be extremely difficult to capture. At the end of the run, Annette is able to gain line and we work the salmon into the frog water. After about ten minutes, the twin to Ellen's fish is in the net.

"Thank you, Lord!", I proclaim for the second time.

We anchor in the calm water, out of the way of the other boats, just as Barb hooks up. Three fish in less than an hour! Amazing! They have her fish boated in about ten minutes, and incredibly, we watch Kevin as he gets his turn. He does a great job, and we have four beauties before 10:00 in the morning.

THE NEXT DAY, THE BEARDSLEYS treat us to a full day Kenai Fjords Wildlife Cruise of Resurrection Bay with a lunch buffet on Fox Island. We wake up early and make the two hour drive to Seward. It is rated as one of the most scenic road trips in Alaska and does not disappoint. We embark on the Nunatak and immediately start to see wildlife— sea otters, dolphins, puffins and even a glimpse of a pod of orcas. Sea Lions and walrus framed by truly stunning scenery, snowcapped mountain peaks and glaciers framed by the deep blue water. Of course, my mind was on the potential fishing opportunity when we explored a small bay with a remote cabin and a skiff tied to its dock. It was a great experience, and something that the wife and I would probably never do on our own.

Kevin and Ellen are in my boat the next day in pursuit of the elusive Kasilof River king salmon. We launch at the ramp just down the road from our house and will take out about seven river miles downstream. We fish the Island Hole, Traps, and the People's Hole without any action. Although we have lots of other boats to keep us company, we only see one fighting a fish. My favorite spot is coming up, and I am hoping that there is no competition for it. There is one guide boat, rowing against the current just below where we want to be, so I maneuver the boat right to the seam where swift and slow water mingle and release the pyramid anchor. This is the "Top of Coho Cove" hole that my Salmon Sensei, Lenny DiPaolo, has shown me. We are using salmon eggs with spin-n-glo attractors attached to planers that dive to the bottom and tap it continuously in the current. Now it is just a waiting game. An hour passes, and nothing happens other than reeling in every fifteen minutes to change bait, and a few nibbles that are probably rainbow trout or dolly varden. Annette had volunteered to stay home today. She often recounts the rainy day that she was trapped fishing with me and our neighbor Marty in this same spot. It was one of those gray days with a steady cold drizzle falling steadily.

She tells it best: "I was sitting there in the freezing wet seat with water drizzling into my rain gear and my head down. I was shivering and more water was dripping off my nose. I'm praying 'Please Lord, let one of them say let's go home.'"

Eventually I did, but it wasn't any too soon for her.

After what seems like an eternity, my rod tip bends a little more than the typical trout bite and then slams down hard. Finally, we have one on! After a few minutes I am convinced that I will not be able to bring the king to the boat against the swift current, so I hand the pole to Kevin and pull anchor. As I row below the fish, Kevin does a great job with the rod. I release the oars, stand up and grab the net. It is dicey— the boat is spinning in the current and heading for a rock, but somehow we get our prize in the net. That was a hard earned king. We are done and call it a day.

BACK AT HOME, I TAKE up a batch of salmon from the smoker, and we consider our options for Thursday. While we were discussing alternatives, our daughter Shannon's black Lab, Lexi, was doing a little counter-surfing, enjoying most of the front row of smoked fish. She took a long nap afterwards. We are thankful that she can't operate a corkscrew.

WE ASKED OUR OTHER friends from Hawaii if they would help us catch some reds, and the Santokis graciously agreed to ferry us to a gravel bar on the bluff above Dot's Fish Camp, on the Kenai River, in Sterling. This was a brand new experience for Kevin and Ellen and they acquitted themselves quite well. The technique is called the Kenai Flip- a yarn fly is attached to a 4-6 foot leader with an ounce of lead and it is flipped upstream and retrieved by pulling the rod with the current in an attempt to hook the migrating sockeye salmon in the mouth. After the sweep is finished, the fly is flipped back upstream. No casting or reeling is involved. When a salmon is hooked it usually makes a leap into the air and then a very powerful run. The fish are strong and plentiful, and we end the day with a bounty to add to the rest of our fish.

WE HAVE BEEN WATCHING the marine forecast religiously, and the next two days are calling for calm winds, flat seas and sunny skies. That means that we have an opportunity for our favorite type of fishing- launching our little Willie boat from the beach into Cook Inlet and fishing for halibut. Ellen and Annette will be in my boat and Kevin will be the third person in Rick's boat. We launch at 7:00 a.m. at low tide, so we have to push the boats about 75 feet down the beach where the water is just beginning to rise as the tide changes. We motor out for ten minutes and drop the anchor in fifty feet of water. I get the girls baited and fishing and then drop my bait down along with the palu bag that allows me to disperse a mixture of ground herring and sand as chum to attract any fish in the area. It isn't long before the girls each get the tips of their rods jiggling. They both hook fish at the same time.

I ask Annette "Is it big?" I should know better.

Her answer is always the same— "I don't know..."

Neither one of the fish is pulling line from the reel, although the rods are bending against their weight. It turns out that the larger of the two is about ten pounds, and big enough for our dinner, so it goes into the cooler. The other is released. We hear a fish flopping in the Larson's cooler, so we know that they have kept one as well. There is a short flurry of action with one more keeper, and then a dry spell.

The day is clear, bright and sunny and I am wearing a short-sleeved shirt, a rarity in our neck of the woods. The girls keep up a steady banter, enjoying the time together and reliving old memories while making new ones. Then Ellen gets very serious as her pole is almost pulled from her hands when a fish hooks itself and runs without the typical prerequisite nibbling action. I don't have to ask how big it is. This one goes directly in the cooler with no questions asked. Shortly afterwards the Blushing Bride adds another, just as big. We don't get our limits today but do end up with a very respectable catch of these delectable denizens of the deep.

I GOT A PARTICIPATION Trophy. We clean the fish on our portable tables at the beach and then head home to vacuum seal and freeze the catch. Kevin helps me clean the boat and reload everything for another halibut adventure. Kevin and Ellen will be fishing with Rick on his boat and James Santoki and his son Jamie will be on mine. We are up early and launch from the beach just as the sun is peeking over the top of the high bluff, painting the sky with azure, peach and golden tones. The glassy water mirrors the hues and promises another glorious sunny and calm day. I point the bow to the snow-capped peak of Augustine and wonder if it's a cloud or if it's smoke that is lingering lazily above it.

I FOLLOW MY HANDHELD GPS to waypoint 14, and James drops the anchor. The chill I feel on the back of my neck is not only from the air temperature; it is a premonition of good things to come. We are near low tide again this morning, so there is very little current, and we are using eight ounces of lead. When the water flow is slack at the tide change, we typically don't get much action, but the fish tend to be bigger for some reason. As the current picks up, the scent from the chum is dispersed more widely, and we get more bites. This day is typical, and we get nothing but tentative nibbles, probably from small fish, for the first hour. Then a more assertive pull is happening on James' rod. He waits just the right amount of time before lifting the rod tip and reeling. In about five minutes, we have a keeper in the box. Then we are in for a flurry of action, with six fish caught in succession— two of them meet our minimum standard, which varies from day-to-day. Then it gets quiet for a while. We hear thumping sounds from Rick's boat and know that he is on the fish as well. There is no significant structure where we fish, so I imagine that the fish roam the seafloor as the buffalo once wandered the plains, grazing on whatever browse is available. When we cut the stomachs of these fish, they are often stuffed with small crabs. I sometimes wonder why they even bite, their stomachs are so full. After our hiatus, I get a signal telegraphed up my line. It is a tentative bite, so I struggle to keep from pulling, and drop my rod tip to the water to give the fish a little slack. When the line tightens, I lift and reel. I am pleasantly surprised with a solid thump and head shaking on the other end. In a few minutes, I make a contribution to the cooler. It is almost time to call it quits, and we have four nice fish in the cooler.

"Fifteen minutes, and we're going in. I'm setting my timer."

The fish perform better when I give them an ultimatum. We each put on fresh baits and drop down, and I scrape the last of the sand and herring chum out of the bucket. Within two minutes of our baits hitting the bottom, Jamie's pole bends double and line is hissing off the reel. This one is not only a keeper, but also a harpooner. After a ten minute tussle, he works the fish to the boat and I drive the point of the harpoon completely through. We get a pretty good shower before I slide it into the cooler. Jamie has the hot rod and gets the catch of the day.

BACK ON SHORE, RICK comes in and they have a limit of nice fish, but he is disappointed.

"We had a real dandy next to the boat, but it came off just as I was about to harpoon it." This is followed shortly afterwards by "But that's fishin'..." We say that a lot in the summer, and it can have a myriad of meanings. Kevin and Ellen are ecstatic with the day and their catch. I hear that halibut taste even better in California.

The Beardsley's adventure is wrapping up, but there is still one more excursion. We are drifting the upper Kasilof from Tustumena Lake down to our house. We will stop at the gravel bar directly across from our house and flip for reds. The upper section of the river has a breathtaking beauty, with no buildings for the first few miles, and then a few remote cabins that can only be reached by water or snow machine in winter. There are riverfront homes on the water for the last few miles, but the scenery is still spectacular. There are two small sections of rapids- just enough to get your heart beating fast, so that you know you are still alive. We launch the boat and park the trailer at the ramp near the outlet of the lake and I row through a mile and a half section known as Slack Water, where the current is almost nonexistent, and the river is wide and shallow. Some of the king salmon spawn in this area and the red salmon migrate through here on their way to where they spawn in the lake, mostly where feeder streams pour into it. Fish jump frequently— big splashes from the kings and smaller ones from the sockeye. One crimson king porpoises twenty yards off the port bow.

"Are we in his court, *The Court of the Crimson King*?", I ask.

At the end of the slow water, we can hear the rushing water of the rapids ahead.

"Can you hear the banjo music from Deliverance?", I ask.

I'm getting giddy and punchy from the marathon non-stop series of adventures. Jimmy Buffet is playing in my head.

And now I must confess, I could use some rest. I can't run at this pace for very long. Yes, it's quite insane; I think it hurts my brain, but it cleans me out and then I can go on...

A flock of ten mergansers takes off next to the boat as we turn the corner and enter the white water. I stay to the left. There are several rocks in this section, and I got to know some of them personally while I was learning to row. The technique for avoiding them is simple: "Point the front of the boat at whatever you don't want to hit and row away from it. Furiously when necessary." I do and we are through the white water in about three minutes. We enjoy the rest of the drift, and I row us to shore at our favorite spot, the gravel bar across from our house. We are extremely blessed to be able to wake up every morning and see the river from our living room, while drinking a cup of coffee. A half mile of the upper Kasilof is visible from the deck. I often tell people "We bought the view. The house came with it." It sometimes freezes completely in our section if we have a week or more of sub-zero temperatures, but it is beautiful every day. Eagles often fly by at eye level and moose are frequent visitors. We clamber out of the boat in our clumsy hip boots and take up positions along the gravel bar. Our river has smaller reds than the Kenai, and our run size, historically, is about half a million fish compared to two million on the Kenai. Consequently, we have much less fishing pressure, and we are okay with that. Have I mentioned that the smaller fish taste better? At any rate, we flail the water for a few hours with limited success, and whoop and holler when we do hook up.

THE SCENERY AND COMPANY are exceptional. All good things come to an end, and this mini-adventure does as well. I row us back across the river, and we tie up to the aluminum landing where our steps lead up the bluff. We trudge the 61 stair steps to the top and stop to catch our breath.

It was a whirlwind exciting series of experiences that we were able to share together, and I'm pretty certain that all of us will need a vacation to recuperate from our vacation.

I don't really care if it does sound corny; I'm gonna say it anyway. We really did have *The Best Time!*

Silvers of September

First published in Alaska Sporting Journal April 2015

F
My blushing bride and I moved from Hawaii to the Great Land in 2009 and have lived on the upper Kasilof River for five years now. During that time, some of the most enjoyable fishing has been for silver salmon. Here are some memorable moments, frozen in time, and the stories that go with them. Our neighbor and my good friend, Lenny DiPaolo, is a former guide on the Kasilof. He has acted as our Salmon Sensei and has given me multiple lessons on where and how to fish the river for each species of salmon. On one trip, he rowed as we approached an area that really didn't look like a "hole". It had no slack water or visible structure that would hold fish.

"There's no fish here!", my better half, Annette, exclaimed with conviction.

Seconds later she ate her words when a powerful strike bent her rod tip to the water. At the other end was an angry silver, which exploded in a geyser of foam. Smiles abounded as Lenny rowed us to calm water and Annette slowly worked the fish to the boat. At the last minute, it peeled line from the reel in one last valiant attempt to escape capture. Finally, we got our silver treasure in the boat. Put the chicken back in the freezer; we are having fresh grilled silver salmon for dinner.

149

WE WERE ANCHORED IN the hole known as Last Chance, not too far above the boat ramp at the bridge where we take out. Lenny was fishing eggs on a light fly rod with a Koa wood butt that a friend and former client from Hawaii built for him. His rod tip began to bounce, and he expertly dipped the tip toward the fish, giving it slack and waiting for an assertive pull before setting the hook. After what seemed like an eternity, he flicked his wrist, and the fight was on! The silver torpedo streaked upstream, jumped twice, and then headed for the fast current in the main river channel. Lenny applied the maximum pressure he could with his fragile wisp of a rod and was able to turn the salmon's head in the right direction. Eventually, his patience and steady pressure won the battle.

JOHN CONLEY AND I LAUNCHED an hour before sunrise and motored toward where Tustumena Lake becomes the Kasilof River. John set a pattern of goldeneye and mallard decoys and I rowed us to shore, where we awaited ducks coming off the lake. After shivering for much too long and watching several flights of mallards fly overhead, oblivious to our decoys, a small flock of goldeneyes came whistling in. John got two, and we had to row after a cripple, which he closed on a couple hundred yards downstream. Rowing back, two more flew in as we were approaching, and he took down another. About an hour later we picked up the decoys and motored back to the launch. John spotted two more ducks on the water, and I "stealth rowed" without taking the oars out of the water, until they were in range. As they flushed, his 12 gauge shotgun boomed once, and we had our first mallard drake of the year.

Then it was time to fish! At the tail end of the Kasilof River's Fourth of July Bar, we back-bounced eggs while anchored in the seam where the current transitioned from fast to slow. I felt the tap-tap-tap of what seemed like a small trout or Dolly Varden bite, but then the rod slammed down, and the reel yielded line grudgingly. A chrome rocket went airborne- once, twice and then three times. Then it was a slow and steady struggle to work the fish to the net. This fish was more streamlined than the silver salmon, had spots on the back and sides, and an iridescent glow of color on its flanks. It was a steelhead buck! After determining that it was deeply hooked, we decided to keep it. Many people fish catch and release only for steelies, while others view the practice as "playing with your food". Everyone agrees that they are an extraordinary game fish. By regulation, anglers may retain two steelhead per year on the Upper Kasilof- above the Sterling Highway bridge. The fish must be recorded on the the back of one's license or harvest ticket. The Kasilof closes for the use of bait on September fifteen, in part to conserve this sub-species of sea-run rainbow trout. *(Steelhead fishing is now only catch and release on the whole river).*

John and I fished three more holes with no results, and then anchored in one of Lenny's favorite spots. I soaked salmon eggs while John cast a large Vibrax spinner within a foot of the bank, retrieving it enticingly- just fast enough to spin the blade. His light spinning rod bent, and he set the hook assertively. It was a respectable hook-nosed buck coho, and we were both smiling. There was a school in the hole and within half an hour I got my limit of two on bait while John caught both of his with his trout- patterned spinner. We were done for the day, and it was a very good day, indeed!

• • • •

OUR DAUGHTER SHANNON and neighbor Craig Allen fished with me the next day. Silvers were definitely coming up the river. We released a steelhead along the first grassy bank and anchored in a hole at the end of the run. One nice fish came into the boat, but other anglers were fishing from the river bank so we moved on. We caught two more fat silvers just above a small creek and kept a steelhead that was bleeding. We are in the last hole, and Craig is drifting eggs downstream under a bobber. At 50 yards downstream, the bobber disappears, and a salmon leaps two full feet above the water and makes a complete 360 degree flip. These are certainly the feistiest fish on the river!

Then it is Shannon's turn. As she back-bounces eggs, suddenly the line goes slack. "Reel, reel, Shanny!" I called out to her. She cranked and a jumbo silver responded with a blistering run. When she finally worked the fish to Craig's net, the buck baptized them into the silver salmon cult by the sprinkling/splashing method. We finished collecting our limits, and then it was time to see who could make their fish look largest by holding it out the furthest. It looked like a tie to me.

MARTY YENTER, FROM Colorado, is our summertime neighbor and went with Annette and I on my first trip rowing our Willie drift boat on the upper Kasilof for silvers. I had fished the river with two former guides and was pretty confident that we could catch limits for everybody without too much effort. After all, I had just been shown all the holes, and the techniques that worked, by two of the best experts. Easy-peasy-lemon-squeezy, right?

Wrong.

Just below the first set of rapids was a slack water that sometimes holds fish. I rowed rhythmically against the current as Annette and our neighbor back bounced clusters of salmon eggs with two ounce sinkers on each side of the boat.

Suddenly Marty yells out "Fish on!"

I wasn't sure who was more surprised- the fish or us. The silver made three slashing runs- upriver and down- and then jumped several times. After a chaotic scene that resembled a *Three Stooges* like sketch involving a net that caught everything but the salmon, the fish was landed. Further on, at the confluence of a small creek, Marty made the hookup announcement again, with gusto. The fish ran downstream, jumped twice, and then headed upstream, tangling with the anchor line. I asked him for the rod, passed it under the rope and handed it back. Miraculously, the fish was still on. Finally, it came to the net and we high-fived triumphantly. Marty managed to land two silver bullets in spite of my inexperience and marginal rowing skills. Annette and I were both skunked. I believe this may have been the last time we fished for silvers with Marty. Nothing personal, buddy...

NOT EVERY FISHING TRIP is a catching trip that ends with the thrill of victory. Our middle daughter, Kris Webber, fished with us on one of those lackluster days. The only thing more frustrating than the "clousy" weather and not getting many bites, is missing multiple strikes. In Hawaii, we would call this having "stink hand" or blame it on having "rubbah hook". After Kris missed her fourth serious bite and reeled in her hook devoid of salmon eggs, I believe that dad may have said a very bad word. Her expression says it all.

THE WEATHER IN SOUTH Central Alaska in September can occasionally be somewhat wet and cool. On one of the last days of the open season for fishing with bait on the Kasilof, I asked a neighbor and fellow expat from Hawaii to fish with me. Bobby Dang has fished the Kasilof for the better part of three decades and ran a bustling lodge back in the heyday, when the hatchery was open, and the fishing was legendary. This was before the unfortunate decline in king salmon runs. Superstitious Hawaiians would never ask if someone wanted to go fishing, for fear that the fish would hear. Instead, they would ask if you want to go "walking around".

"You like go holo-holo?" I asked, lapsing into pidgin English. "Rain, rain, but we no going melt."

"We go!", he responded enthusiastically.

And we did. The fish didn't care that it was raining, but we were down to the last three holes with nothing in the box to show for our efforts. Bobby and I were cold and wet, and he suggested that we go in already.

"Not until we get our fish", I said.

We were at a slough at the end of a grassy bank, just below the lodge where he lived. Finally, a tentative bite turned into silver flash at the end of his line.

"Hanapa'a, hookup!", I yelled.

This fish was not a trophy by any means, but some of us believe the smaller fish are tastier. At least that's what we say when we catch one. We were able to put one more fish in the box at Last Chance. Then we each had a fine fresh fish dinner after a hot shower chased the chill from our bones.

THE LAST DAY WE FISHED this year was a family affair with Shannon and Annette on board. I find myself thinking *"I sure hope they don't see this story in Hawaii. It's already getting a little too crowded here!"*

2019 Okinawa, Japan.

It was the best of times... I am two years old. My father, who is in the Air Force, is transferred from West Palm Beach, Florida to Naha, Okinawa. My mother, two older sisters and I travelled on the SS Breckenridge, with a brief stop in the port of Honolulu, Hawaii. I have vague memories, probably fortified with old photographs, of palm trees and my sisters modeling their flower lei like movie starlets. My most vivid memory is hanging on to the crepe paper streamers that were thrown from the dock to the boat. The longest ones dangled all the way to the surface of the water, and I was fully convinced that if I held onto it long enough, I could catch a fish. Sixty some years later, we find ourselves flying to Okinawa via Honolulu to visit our daughter and son-in-law, who is also in the Air Force. We are ecstatic to reunite with our nine year old granddaughter and six year old twin grandsons. History may not always repeat itself, but it certainly rhymes.

OF COURSE, I SCHEDULE a fishing trip. We meet our Japanese Captain and English speaking deckhand, Jeremy. He is a burly and very personable character, originally from Washington, and he has experienced working on a boat in Alaska. The boat we will be going on is a commercial fishing sampan that is used on weekends to transport charter anglers to the Fish Aggregating Devices anchored to the seafloor, about a two hour ride from the harbor in Kin. The boat owners pay a fee to an association that deploys and maintains the FADs. My son in law, John, will be fishing with me. We are joined by a cadre of about ten marines and their gregarious Gunnery Sergeant. The method of fishing consists of chumming the area next to the buoy by tossing out handfuls of tiny baitfish and drifting out the two inch baits with a surprisingly small hook and light lead. The primary target is the small tuna that usually hang out in proximity to the structure. They come and go in concert with the existence of their food prey and their predators— marlin, larger tuna and fishermen. There can also be an assortment of trigger fish, rainbow runner, mahi, and wahoo at times. The price of the basic trip is very reasonable, and there are two additional options offered. The first is to use deep water jigging gear to target larger tuna that are usually found deeper in the water column. The cost for this is an additional twenty dollars. For forty dollars more, an angler is assigned one of the four trolling rods used while traveling to, from, and in between the various buoys. John is signed up for the deep jigging, and I opt for the full experience.

We steam out of the harbor just as the sun is rising. It is damp and a chill is in the air, but the seas are calm. One hour out, the waves increase to to a gentle swell, but there are no whitecaps. No action on the trolling rods, and no birds in sight. The diesel engines thrum steadily. Finally, the buoy comes into sight and our sleepy crew begins to stir. Jeremy hands out rods and distributes small boxes of the slightly thawed minnows. My rig doesn't have a weight, but he says that it may be better that way. I worry about the breeze blowing it into another line but tell him I'll try it. Our skipper positions the boat for the first drift by the FAD and gives the signal for us to start fishing. The first few handfuls of chum are thrown, and the water is lit up by electric black, gold and silver flashes just below the surface. I thread the point of the hook through the eye sockets of two of the baitfish and drift them out in free spool while feathering the spool with my thumb, to prevent a backlash. Suddenly the line grows taut, and I engage the clutch. It fights as valiantly as a three pound 'ahi can but is overcome quickly with the heavy gear. John has one at the boat, also. We have dinner! That's always a good thing to achieve. There was a very popular television commercial for a bank in Hawaii that had a fisherman calling his wife from a boat, saying "Put the chicken back in the freezer; we got some fish!" Fishing is not always catching...

We run our lines back out and John is rewarded with another juvenile tuna, this time it has the dark blue lines of a small skipjack— aku in Hawaiian. I am robbed of bait without a hookup. The marines are marking their catch with various colors of zip ties attached just above the tail, but we are clipping the tip of the top tail fin to identify ours when they come out of the live well. Nobody else is catching, so the captain runs us back up in position and gives the signal to start fishing. I'm pretty happy with the way my bait drifts back naturally without the lead weight. This drift goes out a little further than the others, before the line goes taut. When it does, the rod bends over assertively, and the reel yields drag. This isn't one of the tiny tuna. Jeremy sees my situation and comes to my aid with the gaff. This 'ahi is more than twice the size of the others. I am very happy and ask John to take a picture. I like this kind of fishing!

On the next drift, John catches another fish, but afterwards he looks a little green behind the gills and decides to take a break. Jeremy tosses more chum, and the tuna come around, but this time a neon blue marlin lights up and crashes through the school. It appears to be well over a hundred pounds. Jeremy instantly grabs one of the freshly caught tuna and bridles it for live bait. A loop of twine is run through the forward part of the eye socket with a bait needle, and both ends of the loop are slid over the tip of a 12/0 hook. The hook is twisted until the line is drawn tight against the head and then the point is tucked under the string so that it is upright between the eyes. He drops it back, and the marlin returns! It lights up with that incredible color again, takes the bait, then turns and runs. I am shaking, watching that display right next to the boat. Jeremy feeds it line, but when he engages the reel, nothing happens. It is heartbreaking. That puts an end to the tuna at this buoy, so the skipper plugs in the coordinates for another FAD a few miles away.

Jeremy sets out the trolling lures, and I get to help under his direction. He likes the Black Bart lures, famous for their effectiveness in Kona. The buoy is in sight, and we are about to pull them in, when the line snaps out of the port outrigger and the rod bends over. It pops back up almost immediately.

"Was that a strike", I ask.

"I'm not sure", he replies.

I tell him "When I'm the deckhand and that happens, Captain Lee always has me run the lure back about ten or fifteen yards and then reel it in quickly. I'll do that two or three times. Sometimes they come back..."

We reel the lures in and stow them in preparation for drifting. This time, we catch a few tunas and Jeremy filets one to cut a chunk of bait which he puts on a larger hook for one of the marines. A few minutes later, a mahi mahi is dancing behind the boat. Two more twelve pounders come to the boat before the flurry of action ends. I try the deep water jigging, but only catch one yellowfin, about the same size as the others. Time keeps on slipping into the future, and always more quickly than usual on a fishing trip. We have had a lot of action, there are a few good meals worth of fish for the family, and we even have a marlin story or two to tell. The drift fishing gear is stowed, and we set out the trolling lures. Within a minute of finishing the final lure adjustments, the long corner rod crashes down with authority, and the reel buzzes with two short pulses. The hair on the back of my neck is standing at full attention as Jeremy drops the lure back and then reels furiously. On the fourth turn of the reel handle, a marlin smashes the lure again and shoots up into the air like a Polaris missile. It looks like it weighs at least 150 pounds. The marines are screaming!

I am frozen and Jeremy yells out "Kajiki!" and whatever words mean "Gas the boat!" in Japanese.

The skipper is enclosed in his cabin, so I run up and repeat "Marlin!" and give the appropriate international hand signals for "Go like hell!"

He understands completely and does. Jeremy assigns the rod to one of our marines while he and I clear lines and stow the rods. The skipper eventually slows the boat, but a lot of line has gone out. The first angler is fighting the fish from the pole holder and begins to lose enthusiasm after about ten minutes. I ask to relieve him, and Jeremy gives his approval. This is a commercial fishing boat, so there is no fighting chair or even a gimbal. My method for fighting fish from the rod holder is to grab the line with a gloved hand below the bottom guide and pull it down to the reel smoothly while reeling, without allowing any slack. This method is slow and steady. Jeremy nods his approval. The fish makes two short line stripping runs on the way back, but the tide is turning in our favor. Each of the four of us have two shifts of five to ten minutes. John somehow rallies from his bout of mal de mer to capture the experience on video.

When the fish is about thirty yards out, the "Gunny" approaches me. "We've talked it over, and want you to take the rod when we have to go to the side of the boat to harpoon it."

"Okay fine", I reply.

I am flattered, and surprised that they want the 66 year old to perform this part of the process. Jeremy fits me with a fighting belt that has a recess where the butt of the rod engages. One of the marines has the line almost up to the leader, so it is Go Time. I take the 130 pound class rig and shuffle over to the starboard side. The fish is angry and scared, and makes a desperate run to the bow of the boat. There is a perilous moment when it tries to go under the keel, where the line would surely be cut, but Jeremy is able to turn it. I retrieve line to the 300 pound test lure leader, and our most excellent deck hand overcomes the valiant last effort of the mighty fish. The skipper plants the harpoon precisely, and the marlin is ours! For me, it is always somewhat bittersweet. It was a Great Fish. The marines are beyond ecstatic, whooping, hollering and hoo-awing, as only Marines can, with unbridled enthusiasm.

The rest of the trip back to the harbor is uneventful. The family is waiting for our return at the pier, and they look puzzled as we pass them by instead of docking. The captain takes us to the next pier, where we can weigh the fish. A mechanical hoist is used to lift the marlin, and it comes in at 112 kilograms-about 250 pounds. It is the skipper's first marlin while fishing with the weekend trips, and he is beaming. Picture taking time, and the marines start to chant *JEREMY-JEREMY-JEREMY* for him to go up. Afterwards, they do the same for me and my face turns red. Then the fish is loaded back on the boat, and we tie up at the dock where Jeremy cuts and distributes the smaller fish to their respective owners.

My blushing bride asks, "What was up with all the name yelling over there?"

"I got to play a pretty substantial part in catching the fish", I reply. "You are still my best catch though." Always sucking up. Don't laugh... it works sometimes.

After all of the small fish are cut and passed out, Jeremy starts on the marlin. His method is different than the way we do it in Hawaii. He saws the carcass into chunks before filleting it, whereas we would leave the carcass whole and filet it in sections after cutting down the centerline. We are given first choice of the meat, and take two of the sections, leaving plenty for the others to share. Our trip was not only a great adventure, but also yielded a great harvest of fresh fish. Smoked marlin is in our near future. We thoroughly enjoy the rest of our vacation with family, exploring the island, playing with the Grands and eating some great local food. It is always hard to say goodbye.

HONOLULU, HAWAII.

Our friends Jicky and Marla have graciously offered us accommodations at the Ferrer Hale for three days on our return trip to Alaska. We are quartered in the Aloha Suite, very tastefully and artfully decorated with Hawaiiana. Jicky is one of a group of young families who we bonded with as first time homebuyers when Waipio Gentry was developed. He was declared "Most Romantic Husband" by the Honolulu Star Bulletin in an essay writing contest. I am hoping to pick up some pointers during our visit.

It was great to have some time to eat tasty local food and reconnect with old neighbors and friends. I called up Captain Lee Severs of the Sea Verse III, and he said that I could go out as a second deck hand with his boat on a 3/4 day six hour charter if I wanted. I jumped on the offer. He is officially retired now and has Captain Mike Duffy running the boat. I'm very excited to accept, and

Annette plans to connect with some of her high school friends and go to lunch that day.

Departure time is 6:15, and I'm early. Many great memories came flooding back during the early morning drive. There was no traffic. Mike has just hired a new deckhand named John, who has experience on boats, but has not worked on a six pack charter boat, so I'm surprised to be the primary hand on a boat that is being run quite differently from the way Lee did. Our charters are two IT techs who are on the island for a seminar and vacation trip. They are right on time. Mike does the briefing in the harbor before we leave. He lays out the lures he wants to run on the fighting chair and explains what goes where. We leave port just as the sun is rising. It's going to be another beautiful day in Paradise with lots of sun and gentle seas.

After I get the lures out, the skipper directs their final placement to his satisfaction. He has just bought a few new ones from another captain who needed some cash and is eager to try them. We are headed to Barber's Point, and beyond for three hours and then he will return for a half day reservation that is scheduled for the afternoon. Charter fishing can be feast or famine, with a generous supply of both. Nothing happens for an hour and a half, and then the long corner and short outrigger rods begin screaming in protest simultaneously. He directs the guys to reel in the fish from the pole holders while we clear the other lines. We manage to get one of the fish aboard— about a twenty pound ono. The other has cut the leader with its razor-sharp teeth. The rubber skirts from the lucky lure are shredded, so we set out two new offerings. Our fishermen ask if he will cut it up for them to take some to eat. Captain Mike looks at the wahoo in the fish box for a long while and has a sober look on his face. "This fish has a serious disease that makes it inedible. You can tell by the prominent stripes on its side. The disease is called 'Crewitis'..."

We have turned the corner around Barber's Point now, with the ever-present associated whitecaps, and are headed to an area where small tunas are known to gather. There is a large flotilla of trailer boats and large charter boats, some of which are drifting and fishing with baits and/or jigs for the tuna. We see a few people hooked up, but most are just fishing. We are almost at the three hour mark, so Captain Mike turns the boat around in a large circle. Just as we are straightening out, the long outrigger snaps loudly and line begins screaming off the reel at an alarming rate. I jump on the rod that is closest to the fish to clear it to avoid tangling, but Mike is yelling something from the bridge.

"Push the drag to the stop!" is what he is saying. The resistance on the 130 International reel was set in the event a smaller fish hit, but we need to increase the drag with something this size. We have a Pacific Blue Marlin hooked, and it announces itself by making four stunning leaps sideways 150 yards from the boat. I assign the stronger looking of our geeks to keep the rod bent and the line tight while we reel in and store the rods. I get him to move to the chair and then deliver the rod, seating the butt in the gimbal. We are beginning to gain line, slowly, when my first angler begins to fade. I order a personnel change and keep the line tight while it happens.

"If this line goes slack, we will lose the fish", I tell them earnestly.

They listen attentively and do their best. The fish makes a short run and then stops.

"You need to turn its head; the line goes out or comes in! If you stall out it will come off!"

These guys have heart, and after two switches back and forth, the leader is getting close. The flying gaff is readied and tied off to the base of the fighting chair, and the large pole gaff hook is in place next to the ladder going up to the bridge. Captain Mike calls John up to relieve him at the controls and slides down the ladder on the rails. Tension is high. Our skipper looks like he is wishing that he had his regular deck hand instead of a greenhorn and another somebody that Captain Lee wanted him to take fishing.

"Can you leader it?", he asks anxiously.

"I can!", I try to say with some level of confidence.

The angler is reeling the swivel up to the rod tip as I grab the leader with my left hand, pull it forward and take a wrap. You only wrap the line around your hand once, because if you do it twice and the fish runs, well... it might not end well. I work my way toward the bow so that the skipper can position himself below me, and he stands ready with the flying gaff up in the air. We are still under power, at about four knots, and the drag on the fish is too much for me. It looks even larger at the boat than it did earlier.

"Go neutral!", I yell up to John, and he does.

As the boat slows, the resistance decreases to the point that I can gain another wrap, and I gain two feet at a time of the twenty foot long 300 pound test leader.

"Forward, slow!", Mike yells upstairs, concerned that the fish might turn under the boat, or into the propeller.

He's the Captain. Our marlin is now ten feet, eight, six, four and then coming up right next to the boat. She rears her head, and the bill comes out of the water, but she isn't able to turn and run. Mike places the gaff precisely just behind the head sinking it deeply as our fish uses the last of its strength. It turns Neon Blue and Silver, pulling the gaff hook free from the handle and stretching the rope tight. Mike pulls it in with the gaff line and I set the second large, fixed gaff through the mouth. Mike uses the weighted bat to administer the death blow, and we have our prize. I open the fish door in the center of the stern, and we slide our trophy in, working in concert with the ocean swells. It takes up most of the back deck. Our two anglers are ecstatic and can hardly process what has happened. Catching a marlin is rare, and doing so on a six hour charter is almost unheard of. We take a few pictures and then fill wet burlap bags halfway with ice and place them on the fish, covering it with a tarp to be able to bring it to market in the best possible condition. Then it's cleanup time, reset the lines, and head for the harbor.

The trip back is uneventful. Aside from seeing a few scattered birds and lots of boats, our ocean is a vast desert. We run up the blue marlin flag and orange ono flag at the head buoy. Captain Lee is waiting for us, and Mike does an excellent job of docking in the narrow channel and berth. A deckhand from the boat next door hands me the bow line as we arrive. *"Bow, spring, stern"*, I chant to myself for the last time on this boat. John has the stern.

"I told you he was lucky", are the first words Lee says to Captain Mike.

"Blessed is better than lucky!" is my response. We've been over this before.

The second half day charter group is waiting anxiously, probably with Great Expectations, so we offload the marlin for a few photos, and then transfer it to Lee's Tundra for the short trip to the auction warehouse. We cover the fish with enough ice to last until the auction on Monday and head back to the boat.

MIKE AND JOHN DEPART with a wave, and my history of adventures on the *Sea Verse, Sea Verse II and Sea Verse III* appears to be coming to a dramatic end. Much like the feeling of capturing a large fish, or harvesting a big game animal, the joy is mixed with sorrow. It is a strange brew of emotions. Captain Lee is uncomfortable when I hug and thank him, but Ido it anyway. This goodbye is particularly difficult. I am exhausted, physically and emotionally, and ready to fight my way back to Mililani in the ever-present traffic for a shower and a beer.

2024
What a great time I have had, putting these stories down and reliving them! Great Adventures are always better in retrospect.

I have crystal clear memories of visiting my Grandpa Misik and fishing in his boat for sheepshead (we called them sergeant-majors) in Fort Pierce, Florida. That's probably the source of the passion I have for the pursuit of fish. I am seven years old, and we have just made the weekend car ride from West Palm Beach to his house. Grandma hugs me and then Grandpa. He has big work-worn hands and smells of Aqua Velva after shave. Entering the house, I smell chicken paprikas on the stove and my mouth is watering.

"Little Char, you want to go out back and see if we have a watermelon that's ripe enough to pick?"

"Sure, grampa, and can we put a penny on the train track?"

"I have one in my pocket. And do you want to go fishing with your cousins tomorrow?"

"Yes, I do!" My joy is complete. And now I'm going to go climb "The Big Tree" until it's time for dinner.

Last summer we had the privilege of having all three of our daughters and all seven of our grandkids, ages one to ten, together in Alaska. It was a wonderful experience, filling our home to bursting with lots of love, joy and people. I was blessed to be able to spend time with each of our grands and I hope that they will have good memories of the time we had together.

My son-in-law John and our two oldest granddaughters had a halibut adventure on one of the last days of their vacation this year. We left the house at zero-dark-thirty to be able to launch near the high tide so that we wouldn't have to push the boat too far down the beach to launch. We are met with blue skies and mirror flat water reflecting the volcanoes across Cook Inlet. The air is brisk and clean. It is almost always brisk in The Great Land. Our little outboard roars to life and we motor out for no more than ten minutes where John drops the anchor in sixty feet of water. The tide is just beginning to ebb, so we can hold bottom with only eight ounces of lead. John and I have rods and the girls will take turns.

"Jun-Ken-Po for who goes first, and then you fish until you catch one or lose your bait. Then it's your cousin's turn."

It isn't too long until Keira gets something jiggling the tip of her rod. It's a classic bite—the little vibration and then a seven second pause—jiggle again and then the pause. "Did it steal my bait, Papa?"

"I don't know; if you pull it too soon it might scare it away and if you wait too long it will steal your bait. When you think it has the herring lift and reel. If it doesn't get hooked, just drop it back down."

On the next nibble, she lifts and reels and exclaims "I got one, papa, I got one!" Sure enough, this one is a keeper.

John asks, "How do you know if it's a keeper?"

"If you're not ashamed to pull it out of the cooler, it's a keeper. We're a little less particular on our standards for the first fish, because we want one for dinner and we are much more particular on our last fish because we want a big one."

Now it's Zoe's turn, and it doesn't take her long to bring one up. It looks like it's about eight pounds. I unhook it and watch it swim away.

We are treated to an exceptional day of fishing that matches the weather, with the cooler filling up. I am cutting bait when I hear John say "Uh-Oh."

"What is it John, what's wrong?"

"I'm getting a bite", he says. In my sixty some years of fishing I have heard many people communicate that they were getting a bite, but this was the first time I heard that.

"It's okay, John, getting a bite is a good thing." He sets the hook at the right time and has a real rod-bender. This one will not be an embarrassment, so it goes directly in the cooler. Zoe is next to pull in a nice one, and then it's my turn. We set the drags fairly tight to be certain that there is enough resistance to drive the point of the hook in when a fish bites. When it pulls line on the way up, we know that it is a good one. This one is taking line.

"Pull up your rigs; this is a big fish. We don't want to get tangled."

Keira is reeling in, so I give my phone to Zoe. "Shoot a video, Zo-zo!" The edited recording is one minute and forty-two seconds long. It should have been shorter.

As the chum bag comes up Keira says, "Come out, come out, come out." I attempt to harpoon it, but my aim is too far forward, and it hits the skull bone causing the fish to pull out another ten yards of line. *"Third Time!"* she says.

"It's really giving you a workout, huh John?"

"Yeah, it is!"

Zoe narrates "We're reeling in this fish so we can make halibut tacos!"

John says, "That's the goal."

Zoe again, "Yes, halibut tacos; that's the ultimate goal."

I do my best Bubba Gump impression. "Halibut tacos...grilled halibut...fried halibut...halibut creole... beer-battered halibut... halibut chowder... halibut curry... halibut Olympia. . ."

"*It's coming; it's coming, it's coming in!*", Zoe interjects.

"Halibut Olympia is the bomb", John says. I have the leader and finally sink the harpoon just forward of the dorsal fin. "Papa got it, papa got it this time, girls; I think it's tired, too. *Nice fish, nice fish!*"

"*Big, big, big boy!*", Zoe agrees.

I use the meat hook and the harpoon line to slide it in the cooler. "Woo-hoo, thank you, Lord!"

Zoe tells Keira "Say bye."

"Bye." And we are done. Memories are made.

This is the end of my stories... for now. I have many more, and hopefully, trunks of memories still to come. Hope for the future. Something we all need.

About the Author

Charley McCrone is a quintessential American. As a GI Brat, he spent the first sixteen years of his life living in New Mexico, Florida, Okinawa, Oklahoma and New York. Graduating from high school, he then lived in Florida, Arkansa and the Blue Ridge Mountains of North Carolina. Thirty five years were spent in Hawaii and the last fifteen in Alaska. After a forty five year career as a tile setter and then a tile contractor, he retired two years ago. He enjoys being retired, hunting and fishing and, apparently, writing. This is his first book.